Lessons from the Prairie

Lessons from the Prairie

The Surprising Secrets to Happiness,
Success, and (Sometimes Just) Survival
I Learned from America's Favorite Show

MELISSA FRANCIS

WEINSTEIN
BOOKS

Printed in the United States of America.
Book design by Jack Lenzo
Set in eleven point Arrus

Library of Congress Cataloging-in-Publication Data is available for this book.

ISBN: 978-1-60286-306-4
E-Book ISBN: 978-1-60286-307-1

Published by Weinstein Books, an imprint of Perseus Books, LLC, a subsidiary of Hachette Book Group, Inc.
www.weinsteinbooks.com

Weinstein Books are available at special discounts for bulk purchases in the U.S. by corporations, institutions and other organizations. For more information, please contact the Special Markets Department at Perseus Books, 2300 Chestnut Street, Suite 200, Philadelphia, PA 19103, call (800) 8104145, ext. 5000, or e-mail special.markets@perseusbooks.com.

First Edition

10 9 8 7 6 5 4 3 2 1

To my three precious jewels:
Thompson, Greyson & Gemma.
We love you to the moon and back.

CONTENTS

The *Little House on the Prairie* One

The red digital clock just beneath the camera lens hits the top of the hour, and I kick off my four-inch, red stilettos faster than you can say hideous bunions. Before I even stand up from the curvy white couch, I slide on my homely (heavenly) orthopedic sneakers and sigh. I'm sure the tourists on the other side of our glass studio windows at Fox News are horrified, but also secretly reveling in the pure humanity that is my ugly, ugly feet. Oh well. Sharing such secrets is the price I pay for working, quite literally, on display.

Like all the big networks these days, Fox has built a street-level studio behind big picture windows that allows fans and tourists to look in on our workspace during the live show and wave manically while we fight about hot topics in bright dresses and fake eyelashes. Most days I feel like a goldfish in a shiny fishbowl. A goldfish who sincerely appreciates that viewers find the spectacle compelling enough to stop by and tap on the glass. Without their interest, I wouldn't have a job! Thank you.

I usually pass unnoticed as I make my way from the studio, through the breezeway, and back to my office, but on this day I'm stopped by two smiling ladies bundled against the cold, holding out comically oversized pens. They look like the writing instruments my kids hand to Mickey Mouse to get his signature at Disney.

"Would you sign this for me?" the pink-coated lady asks, pressing a piece of paper into my hands.

"I'd be happy to," I say. "But I think you'll be disappointed when you read my name. The ladies coming right behind me are a lot more famous. You should wait for one of them."

"Oh, no. We know who you are. You're Melissa Francis," the second lady says, handing me her own pen and paper. "You're the *Little House on the Prairie* one! I grew up with you."

The *Little House on the Prairie* one . . .

I never think of myself as the *Little House on the Prairie* one, and I'm still taken aback when people remember me from that time. Decades later (please don't stop to do the math—I can't take it), most people recognize me as a television journalist, but I grew up in Hollywood, smiling for the camera before my first birthday. From sudsing my hair in an infant tub to sell Johnson & Johnson Baby Shampoo, to hawking (cold, painted) hamburgers for McDonald's, to more serious turns in dramas, I worked pretty steadily from the time I was a baby though my teenage years. I was probably best known as Cassandra Cooper Ingalls, Michael Landon's adopted daughter on *Little House on the Prairie*. Pa adopted my TV brother, Jason Bateman, and me after a violent covered-wagon accident pulverized our natural parents right before our very eyes.

For those of you too young to remember—or others who are unfamiliar with the concept of television or *People* magazine—*Little House on the Prairie* was a wholesome family drama broadcast during the late seventies and early eighties that was set a hundred years earlier in the small prairie town of Walnut Grove, Minnesota. We rode around in wagons pulled by horses, mostly grew our own food, and lived in a tiny wooden house that lacked plumbing.

Just as a side note, after I showed my sons the show and pointed to myself as the child on the screen with a bonnet and long brown braids sitting in the back of the wagon, they naturally assumed I grew up in a time before cars were invented and continued to carry that idea with them and share the notion with friends despite my protests to the contrary. Which is not terribly flattering in my business, where age really counts. They also asked at what age their hair would turn spontaneously blonde like mine obviously had.

But I digress.

The show was based on the best-selling series of Little House books by Laura Ingalls Wilder, which still reign as timeless, go-to children's literature, having hit the must-read list long before Harry Potter or Katniss Everdeen ever inspired legions of fans. I must tell you, these colorful, historic stories still hold up. I took the whole series on vacation, and other than the predictable fact that Charles never dies at the hands of the grizzly bear/furious Native American/storm of the century, they are wildly entertaining, and one can easily understand why countless readers have put themselves in the rough boots and stockings of those who grew up on the prairie in the mid-1800s and experienced the rigors of farm life on the frontier firsthand. What blows me away is that the hardscrabble stories of life on the very edge of civilization are supposedly true! I have to hand it to Laura Ingalls Wilder: even if she did exaggerate a bit here and there, or her daughter did when she filled out the stories in her mother's advancing years, the content is staggering. I never would have survived for more than a week on the prairie. Lord knows I need a hot bath and a glass of Mommy's Time Out at the end of a long day or I'm no good to anyone in the morning.

For years, *Little House* was one of the top-rated shows on television, one of the tent poles of the NBC prime-time lineup. You can imagine the impact of being a hit in the 1970s and '80s, when people had perhaps six or seven working channels at best. And no Internet. And no Facebook. Or smart phones. So you could basically watch one of half a dozen shows on TV or play a board game. I guess you could read. But you get my point.

A lot of kids at my school watched *Little House*, which also starred Melissa Gilbert, Melissa Sue Anderson, and Karen Grassle. However, in our house, the show was on past my bedtime, so I had never seen that covered wagon roll into the tall grass of the prairie during the opening credits, or watched the girl who played Carrie wipe out while running down the hill and then stand up and looked dazed, as if she'd hit her head a bit too hard. My sister and I were overscheduled children before that was a thing, and my mother was absolutely *done* with us by 8:00 p.m., so Tiffany and I were always bathed, scrubbed, and tucked in by then. I had never seen 8:01 and had no idea primetime television existed.

That's why, when I got a call for the audition, I gave the whole thing one big yawn. Another day, another audition, nothing to see here. Except this bunch of freaks used odd language like "Ma" and "Pa" and "reckon."

"Maybe I will just change that when I go in and say something more believable like, 'Mom,'" I mulled over while reading the sides (sides are the little fraction of a scene they give you for the tryout so you don't walk out the door with too much information about what's coming up on the show and blab the juicy details to the world).

"No, no, no," my mother said with her terrifying, trademark force. "Stick to the script! These people lived, I don't know, like in the 1800s. Pioneers and covered wagons and all that. You've seen pictures in school. They all had horses; you love horses. Think horses. Do well and you'll get a horse. Think horses."

Yes, horses.

Mmmmm, horses. Little girls do love horses.

Wait, where was I?

My mother was wound tight as a top for this audition. Her normal audition swagger had a hitch. We used to joke that the other kids sitting in the waiting room, going over their sides, had "wasted their gas." That was our code for: I'm getting this job, just how I got so many others.

This time, she looked less sure.

She said, "You really need to do well on this one."

I thought I had to do well on *every* audition. Why was this one any different? Whatever. Where was my horse anyway?

When I strolled into the room to audition, Michael Landon was there. I didn't know who he was, but I could tell by the energy in the room that he was an important person. There were probably four or five other people in the room with us. My mother was on the other side of the door, biting her nails with the other stage moms—*willing* me to get the part. But even at eight years old, never having seen the show, I could immediately tell that Michael Landon was a force. He filled the room. He had an undeniable star quality. His energy electrified the air the moment he laughed at my wide eyes, framed by long ropes of brown braids that (God and my mother willing!) would be right at home in Walnut Grove.

"So you're Missy?" he boomed, with a wide grin.

Understand, I still had no idea who he was. I'd never even seen a picture of him or seen him on TV that I could remember. But that room suddenly felt like Christmas, and that man was certainly Santa.

We did two scenes together. One was run of the mill, a back and forth at the dinner table. The second called for me to work my signature magic: cry on cue. And I didn't just *cry*—I shed real tears, having just smiled and greeted everyone minutes before. Few kids could pull off this feat. The level of difficulty for an eight-year-old, alone in a room with strangers, just cold one line into a scene, was up there with climbing Mount Kilimanjaro and running a marathon. In the same day. But *this* was what I did. I was perhaps the only girl under ten on the audition circuit who could jump into character and turn on the waterworks from a standing start. This trick was my forte.

I dug in as Michael read the first few lines looking at my face to see what I could muster. Then I hit the gas. I pictured my parents rolling off the side of a hill in their covered wagon as the wood smashed into splinters, the canvas shredding to ribbons, killing my ma and pa and a team of horses to boot. Then I cheated (this is not really kosher in acting) and pictured my real cat and dog in the back, flying into the air and

then crashing down, their bones shattering with every
blow. Then I added my goldfish, King Neptune, whose
bowl smashed into shards in my imagination, while
water splashed all over and he gasped and choked on
the air. The carnage!

I wailed and let loose howling. Poor Princess! And
K.C.! And poor King Neptune! Not King Neptune!

And that was that.

I crushed it. Totally owned the scene. I knew because a nice lady in the room offered me tissues, and
Michael smiled from ear to ear at my misery.

I strutted from the room and out the door, letting
my mother trail me from the building, desperate for
details. I thought the whole ball of wax had gone fairly
well, but I'd learned not to dwell on an audition after
I'd said thank you and hopped back in our family's
brown station wagon to make the long journey back
deep into the Valley. Even I knew the vagaries of casting were impossible to predict.

On the way home, my mother was full of questions. I never wanted to talk when she was like this.
There was so much power in holding back.

"Was Michael Landon inside?" she wanted to know.

"Who?" I asked, uninterested.

"Michael Landon," she repeated with more force,
wanting to strangle me, but not daring when it seemed
I could very well be the proverbial goose getting ready
to lay that precious golden egg.

"Pa! The star of the show."

"I don't know," I said—and, honestly, I didn't. Was that man him? Probably, but who knew? I'm sure he'd told me his name, but I'd been too focused on the flood of tears ahead to absorb that detail. Now I was focused on getting home to make sure all my pets were still alive.

She tried to describe him: "Longish brown curly hair. Haaaaandsome."

Handsome? At his age? He had to be older than my mother, for sure. Handsome? Forget it! She was nuts.

When I got a callback, my mother was over the moon with excitement. She was practically vibrating with anticipation. By this point, I'd stayed up late to watch an episode of the show. I sat on the big chair in front of the television in the living room, with Princess in my lap, and I realized this opportunity was *enormous.*

So I immediately began negotiating.

I said to my mother, "If I get this, can I have a new bridle for Felina?" She was the dapple gray mare I rode on the weekends. See, I was thinking horses, just as she suggested.

My mother said, "Yes, any brand you like."

She would have said anything to ensure I'd be wearing my serious game face, which is why I had already blown off her original pony promise—even though in truth, I didn't need the extra incentive. I always played to win. I was incapable of throwing an audition. I had no problem walking into a roomful of strangers and finding a way to shine. That's how you charm your way through the process and land all those parts. You learn to walk into a room and just *own that bitch*.

I got the part (and the bridle), but at this point the show was limping along on its last legs. Most of the children, like Laura and her sister Mary, along with their nemesis, Nellie, had grown up. Frantically, the producers scrambled to reinject some youth and energy into the show (read: get ratings back where they used to be). Their solution was to round up a fresh batch of kids and find some ways in the storyline to keep them connected to Ma and Pa Ingalls. That's where I came in—me and a young Jason Bateman in one of his early television roles. We were cast as sister and brother, Cassandra and James Cooper.

Let me just take a moment to mention that I thought I had completely hit the jackpot. Here's this older boy, with shiny red hair cut in a straight line across his forehead and dreamy freckles. And we did every scene together. And he was almost always forced to hold my hand! And occasionally hug me! Who needed a pony? This was way better!

Our introductory episode was set around that horrific wagon accident from the audition. Tragically—and inevitably, I guess, given the producers' agenda—my character's parents were killed, and after a few plot twists and turns the Ingalls adopted Cassandra and James. Lucky us! Plus there was a ton of hand holding along the way (yes!).

These new developments allowed the writers to come up with a new batch of stories involving young children—a huge part of the *Little House* formula. And by a new batch of stories, I mean they went back and dug the old scripts out of some dusty filing cabinet somewhere and used White Out to blot the names and scribble in new ones. Then we reprised the old conflict that existed in the earlier episodes between Laura Ingalls and her arch nemesis, Nellie Oleson, played by an actress named Alison Arngrim. If you remember, there was a constant tug and pull between those characters, which in the not-so-subtle ways of prime-time network television came across as the conflict between good and evil. This time around, my Cassandra character would go up against a character called Nancy, an adopted daughter of the Olesons', played by Allison Balson.

The only thing they really changed was that Nancy Oleson would turn out to be even more scheming and dastardly than Nellie Oleson. Cassandra wasn't quite as angelic as Laura Ingalls, but the rest was pretty much the same and everyone was happy: audience, Michael, me (and, obviously, my mother).

Nearly a decade after the show ended its historic run, I decided to leave Hollywood behind and boarded a plane to Boston to study economics at Harvard University. I never really looked back. Oh, I carried the baggage of my hard-charging, toughened-by-rejection, always-striving career as a child actress right onboard that plane with me, but I was done chasing that particular dream. I wanted to try on a life without acting, without the inconsistent joy, without the endless uncertainty, without my controlling stage mother pushing all those buttons behind the scenes. I tried to leave that part of my life at the curb for morning pickup right next to the recyclable cans and plastic.

But you can't really do that, can you?

With age and time, I built a new life. I'm now intensely grateful to have a husband who is loving beyond all measure, and together we have three ridiculous children, who make a deafening amount of noise and light up our lives in the process. I've also built an entirely different career.

Okay, I know what you're thinking: "You're still on television, lady. Entirely different career? Who the hell are you kidding?"

Yes, I'm aware of the irony. I have traveled a great distance in (physical and mental) space and time to do . . . almost the same thing. I guess that can only mean that I have a pathological need to be on television. At least I can admit it. That counts for something! Besides, I have so many issues to tackle in therapy, there really aren't enough hours or doctors. So perhaps you will indulge me and believe that for me, this job is vastly different. For one thing, no one is putting words in my mouth, and that suits me a whole lot better.

But just when I think I'm a completely new person, someone calls me the *Little House on the Prairie* one. I'm still stunned when people remember that part of my life and tell me "that was the only show my mom let me watch." Television goddess Megyn Kelly among them! I remember the first time we met at Fox, and I was such a huge fan, I called her Kelly. As in, "Hi Kelly! I'm a huge fan! Great to meet you!" She must have thought, *What a jackass this girl is.* (I'm getting hives on my neck reliving this story. I wish I were kidding.)

Megyn was of course completely gracious and acted as if she didn't hear my moronic error. And just when I thought I could slink away and reintroduce myself, maybe ten years in the future, when the mortification wore off, she mentioned that, yep, she had watched every episode and knew exactly who I was.

Holy disaster, Batman.

The irony for me is that in the determined process to try to reinvent myself, I failed to embrace the value of where I'd come from. Oprah, the Confucius of our time, says, "No experience is wasted." In fact, what I learned in front of the camera and behind the scenes on *Little House* laid the very foundation and provided the essential tools to build a happy, meaningful life today. For example, who could ever be more resilient than the pioneering Ingalls? Instead of just lying down in the dusty road and letting the next wagon that rolled by put them out of their misery when their crop failed for the fiftieth time, they found, deep inside, the strength to pull up their petticoats and soldier on to better times. In real life, Michael Landon personified that same pioneering spirit as a master of reinvention, repackaging himself on one hit show after another, that he was clever and industrious enough to own and operate as his unique and highly profitable cottage industry.

The *Little House* experience taught me, among other things, to dig deep to find the strength to always fight on another day, sometimes reinventing myself in the process; that good guys really do win in the end, even though they may not always lead at the turn; that motherhood is not for sissies; to identify and chase my passion without letting myself be distracted by fear; and to believe in miracles.

For me, that makeshift set, deep in the Simi Valley under the scorching sun, was in truth a priceless training ground. There was a lot of wisdom in the air—as if the horses kicked up bits of brilliance, not just California dirt—that settled over my shoulders and helped to guide me in the years that followed. If you read on and take this ride with me, I promise to sprinkle a little of that magic on your head, too.

CHAPTER ONE

YOU JUST CAN'T KILL ME (AT LEAST NOT WITHOUT A SERIOUS WEAPON)

W hen my first book was coming out, Melissa Gilbert offered to meet for dinner and fill me in on the unexpected joy and torture that would be The Book Tour. This meeting was like having a date with your kindergarten boyfriend thirty years later. I teased and curled my hair five or six times, and then got right in the shower and started over from scratch.

Melissa is truly the keeper of the *Little House* fan base and heritage, and she has no reason to share, unless you believe that good deeds recycle themselves in the universe.

We met for dinner at her hotel near Gramercy Park, and I had that bizarre experience when someone you haven't seen forever is instantly familiar, as if no time has gone by at all. Voices always stick in my memory. I can think of someone and immediately hear the pitch and melody of their speech. Of course anyone who's watched *Little House* knows Melissa's voice because she was the narrator, but seeing her (and hearing her) in person is still somewhat mind-blowing. The candy-apple-sweet lisp that talked over the frames of so many childhoods was suddenly asking me what I felt like ordering for dinner.

She sat in a chair and folded her legs underneath her like a middle school friend who wanted to gossip about boys. I was a child again. My chest tightened. Here was a once-in-a-lifetime chance to see if my behind-the-scenes memories matched hers. In my head, the chatter and play that happened in the dark corners of the studio and unlit sets, and the action and lines of the scenes that still ran daily in reruns on the cable dial—all of this smashed together on one reel of film that played in my mind's eye.

We had identical memories of how Michael treated us as tiny professionals when we came to work. Although she calls him Mike, and I wonder if I was the only kid saying Michael.

"We were there to work," she laughed. "I remember not knowing my lines once. Once. He got so mad, but quietly mad, scary mad, and sent me away to learn those lines and come back when I could do it right. It wasn't funny. I remember that. I did not do that again."

I told Melissa about the time I accidentally wore my retainer while we were shooting a scene. The orthodontist said to wear the painful piece of plastic every single second that I could when I wasn't shooting. So I wore it between takes, which was begging for disaster. Inevitably I forgot to take it out, and when I told my mom, she immediately marched me to Michael to confess. I was so embarrassed, and plainly terrified. They were already breaking down for the next shot, and I had blown it.

Hearing this story, Melissa clapped her hand over her mouth with a gasp. The shame of our ancient blunders burned as hot as if we were still right there on the set, in the blazing Southern California heat.

"He ran a tight ship. Very tight. We had fun, so many pranks!" Melissa and I reminisced about all the times he shocked the kids on set by taking off his big hat and revealing a giant hairy tarantula—that he then let walk down his face—or scooping up a filthy frog and letting it jump out of his mouth when he spoke. "Yuck! But then when he called action . . . he was no joke," I said.

"But you waited tables and worked in the back of kitchens . . . after *Little House*. After acting. That's a major pay cut. And, you know, humbling. I was surprised to read that about you. That's . . . well, I respect that. I don't know how many kids from back then would do the same thing once they had a taste of the big time," she confessed.

"You are so universally recognizable it would have caused quite a tabloid stir if you stopped by someone's table in a uniform to ask how they like their eggs," I joked.

She laughed. But I knew Melissa was just as much of a fighter. I've seen her in a commercial break during one of my shows selling skin cream that promises to reduce creping (I bought a tube), on the same day I was flipping through her new cookbook. She's magnificent at finding an opening to cleverly capitalize on what's hot. I love that about her.

"Maybe Michael knew how to pick worker-bee kids," I went on. "Or maybe we learned watching him work himself to death every day. Perhaps a bit of both. Either way, we all graduated from his care as nose-to-the-grindstone workers."

"I think that's why none of us ended up in rehab or sticking up a convenience store," she said. "I don't think any of us could stand the thought of him seeing our mug shot."

I think Half-Pint was onto something.

→═◎ ◎═←

"Melissa Francis is live in Concord with the latest on that story . . ."

That was my cue. I stared into the camera lens, a black abyss that sucked the breath from my body. I could hear my photographer's boots as he shifted behind the camera, waiting.

Nothing else.

This moment was exactly what I'd worked so hard for, fought for . . . cajoled, stretched the truth, charmed, and begged for . . .

And I was choking.

Big time.

I'd done so much to claw my way to this opportunity. I'd taken enormous gambles, like chucking a childhood acting career into the waste bin and moving as far across the country as I possibly could. I had spread out my college acceptance letters on the kitchen table and picked Harvard not for the name (I swear) but for the physical distance from Hollywood (2,986 miles by car). I didn't want to be tempted by a smooth-talking agent or strong-armed by my mother to pop back into town for a quick audition. A five-hour plane ride clear across the continent hung up the phone on that conversation. I was going cold turkey on Hollywood.

During that first brisk fall, I trudged through Harvard Yard, crunching pumpkin-colored leaves under my new lace-up duck boots, and, just like Reese Witherspoon in *Legally Blonde*, I gaped in delighted awe at the centuries-old dorms. I thought about what I might transform myself into in the future and what to study to get there. The choices were dazzling: Near Eastern Religion, Romance Languages, Frozen Heroes, Plant Sex! All very tempting.

Ultimately, the Economics Department seemed the right fit. Dissecting the country's balance sheet, studying what breathed life into an expansion and what hobbled a healthy economic growth spurt appealed to my curiosity and my sense of order (plus I'm a huge nerd).

I was drawn to politics, but here the debate from both sides would be sorted, organized, and reasoned with math. Proof. Using unbiased, hard numbers to prove or disprove political theory? I loved the very idea.

When I went to look for a summer internship after my freshman year, though, I knew I didn't want to sit at a desk every day. My first career, my first lifetime, had been spent under the dazzling lights of the entertainment industry, in front of the camera. Earning a paycheck now in front of a computer wouldn't hold my attention for long. I had been spoiled by a life where people seemed to believe that what I did held a kind of magic, even if I knew better. I couldn't quietly type up reports in a dimly lit cubicle now.

I'd gone to the Career Counseling Office and flipped through the black three-ring binders filled with postings for summer interns. Consultants, analysts. I wasn't totally sure what I was qualified to analyze at this point. A listing in the fortieth binder caught my attention: KTTV, the local Fox affiliate in Los Angeles, was looking for an intern to hop on the assignment desk, with an ear to the police scanner and an eye on the breaking news wires. Keeping track of the reporters! Making sure the show producers had the latest updates on raging fires and high-speed car chases! Greasing the wheels of production as the entire machine careens toward show time! This held promise.

And I thought, *They'll let me do that for free? I don't even have to pay for the education? What luck!*

I worked that summer with the station's assignment manager, Carol Breshears. With her elegant
dress and spectacles perched on her nose when they
weren't dangling from a chain around her neck, she
sliced through the day's events with the precision of
a hibachi chef, dicing and sorting the mouth-watering
stories to one side, while pushing the bland and mun-
dane gristle to the other. Carol showed me what to
look for, what made a story sizzle, and where to find
the flaws. She was the first person who ever gave me a
break in news, and she shared her file folder of secrets.
I love her dearly to this day. And I'm so touched every
year on my birthday when she remembers the date
and sends yellow roses, a reminder of our connection.

I caught the news bug that summer working for
Carol at KTTV. And in the summers that followed,
I hunted down facts and interviewed people on the
street for *NBC Nightly News*, pitched stories to the
Today Show from the network's Washington, DC, bureau, and collected sound bites for PBS business and
economics correspondent Paul Solman.

During my last year at Harvard, I put together a
résumé tape, using fast clips from each of those stops.
I'd cajoled photogs at each shop into letting me jump
in front of the lens when the real reporter on our team
was chasing down a sandwich. I made a few dozen
dubs of the compilation that resulted, and paired them
with my skinny little résumé of academic achievements and internships. Then I mailed the bulky

packages to small news markets around the country and waited.

I sat next to my phone, filled with bright-eyed optimism. But all I heard was sound of the icicles that melted from the roof of my dorm crashing to the sidewalk below like so much hope. My fellow classmates landed one plum job after another, getting accepted to top law schools or multiple offers on Wall Street, while I was left to worry if I would ever find work in my chosen field. Panic was beginning to set in. I'd taken a huge flier on the idea of chucking acting and pursuing a far-fetched career that Harvard didn't offer any training to support. No wonder no one else in the class appeared to be skipping down this path with me.

I suddenly felt more than a little bit doomed. If I'd been on *Little House* at that moment, the editors would have cued the super subtle, dramatic music with slow foreboding keys that signaled disaster juuuuust around the corner. Exactly like when Jason Bateman and I joined the show, and our parents, the Coopers, were killed off within minutes of the opening credits, driving their horse-drawn wagon down a steep hill. All the viewer had to do was listen to the music to know who was going to end up happy as a kitten on catnip and who was going to get pulverized into woodchips. The chorus is all joyful strings and horns as Michael Landon drives his team down the hill with Jason and me in tow, then suddenly turns dark, with ominous tension for my poor, doomed parents in the wagon behind us. Sure enough, as the Coopers begin their descent, the wagon goes flying, tumbling out of control, Ma screams, and they are toast. Well, croutons, really.

In order to shoot the scene, the stunt coordinators actually sent an empty wagon down this steep hill, with dummies done up inside to look like Mr. and Mrs. Cooper. The director kept the camera close, focused on the body of the wagon, so the viewers couldn't see that while we shot this particular version of the scene, there were no horses pulling the wagon and thus attached when the wagon finally gets flung off the side of the hill. PETA generally frowns on killing animals in the making of entertainment or television. (Fun side note: Michael Landon loved to use twins of everything when he was shooting, including kids and horses, to save time and money. So no surprise, there were two teams of horses that played the roles of Pa's horses, though being a horsewoman myself, I thought the two different teams of geldings looked nothing alike. The random white markings on their legs and faces were in totally different spots. What a joke! I always wondered if the audience noticed that kind of discontinuity.)

Next the cameras turned to tight shots of Jason and me. I immediately went into my trademark flood of tears, imagining my parents tumbling to their splintered death in front of me—but underneath my sobbing should have been tears of joy. That was the joke I used to tell my friends, when they said how sad they'd been watching me cry as my parents perished. Yes, for poor little Cassandra Cooper, that day was devastating. But for me, the "disaster" ushered in one of the best roles of my life. If the Coopers hadn't tumbled to their untimely death, I wouldn't have become an Ingalls.

A macabre way to illustrate the lesson. But there's the moral of the story nonetheless. We've all taken a header over the side of a cliff now and again. Maybe not as severely as the poor, dead Coopers. More like when Carrie goes ass over teakettle in the opening credits. There's no shame in wiping out. Happens to the best of us. And more than once. But scraping your broken bones up off the prairie floor, summoning your courage and strength, and moving on to fight another day is what separates the weak from the strong.

Plus there's a bonus to having lived through a truly bruising experience: you see that you survived. You know you've battled back from bitter defeat. So the next time life knocks you to your knees, you can look back, and know in your heart you do in fact have the strength and fortitude to overcome once again.

That's powerful.

That's liberating.

I'd experienced a death of sorts when my acting career began to evaporate in my teenage years, but rather than bottom out, head to rehab, or rob a dry cleaners, I'd found a rebirth, a new path forward, at Harvard. Now I had to keep reinventing to find a new career.

⤙⬤⤚

Back in first grade, we used to stand in a long line on the playground during outside recess, so that two designated captains could look us over, head to toe, and pick members of their co-ed kickball teams. There was one girl whose mom let her have too many Hostess Apple Fruit Pies in her lunch every day. The "Real Fruit Filling" seemed to slow her down going round the bases. This poor girl always got picked close to the last, but that's not the embarrassing part. We've all known someone in those shoes (or been there ourselves).

One day, yet again, the choices had dwindled to her and one other very short boy with thick, Coke-bottle glasses. The other twenty-two of us were already selected. And just as one of the team captains was very slowly deciding which of the two would hurt his team the least, the elastic around the waist Hostess Fruit Pie's white cotton slip snapped, and what seemed like yards of fabric tumbled from underneath her skirt to gathered around her ankles.

My heart broke for her, and I remember crying tears with her even though we weren't particularly good friends, as I tried to help her escape the heaped fabric without tripping, so she could run to the nurse's office and hide. She'd sobbed until she couldn't breathe, and her mother had to come pick her up from school. I wasn't sure we'd ever see her at school again.

Fifteen or so years later, in Cambridge now, I felt almost as tripped up as she had. I lay in my dorm room bed on top of my bedspread, wondering if I'd ever get picked for an (employment) team.

Suddenly, I was struck by an idea (well, it was more like a marginally ethical scheme).

I leapt to my feet and picked up the phone. Then I scanned the tidy list of target television news stations I'd made that were within driving distance from Cambridge, and I dialed the news director of the ABC station in Portland, Maine. I hung up after one ring and tried once again to gather my nerve. On the second try, I got through to his assistant and explained that I was coming to his town that Thursday to interview with the competition, and while I was there, I wanted to stop by, deliver a copy of my résumé tape, and perhaps just say hello.

This was, sort of, a complete fabrication.

"If he has a moment," I said, "I thought it might make sense to at least drop off my material while I'm in town anyway for my other interview." I tried to sound casual, like the offer was more to the news director's advantage than mine. What boss in his right mind wouldn't want to at least see the candidate the competition was considering?

The receptionist left me on hold to think about what I'd done. Part of me worried she was calling her best girlfriend who happened to work at that competing station and checking my story.

Luckily, she instead came back after five agonizingly long minutes and told me to feel free to stop by—no promises that I would actually get to meet with anyone—but I was welcome to leave my materials. The temptation I had invented from thin air proved too much to resist!

Now the story about why I was coming to town was true. Giddy with anticipation and cackling like Boris and Natasha advancing a clever plot, I called the other stations in town with the same pitch. I figured if anyone ever called me on the ruse, I would admit exactly what I'd done, with pride, and then ask them if they needed a reporter who could think quickly on her feet to get in the door and gain access to a subject who needed to be interviewed. Amazingly, no one ever questioned me on the tactic, even though I used the trick at least a dozen times that spring.

By the day of graduation, the NBC station in Portland, Maine, had hired me to cut tape, rip scripts, and run the teleprompter for their brand new newscast every weekday at noon. The news director said he could only hire me part-time, and that the position paid $6.10 an hour, minimum wage at the time. But he promised that because this gig was part-time, I would have plenty of time to work on improving my reel after the show every day, and I would be right there, first in line to apply, when a reporter job opened up.

I had an official job in television news! I was on my way.

Of course, not only was I making far less than my classmates who were heading to Wall Street, I also had the distinction of being the only person in the entire graduating class to be moving to Maine. My parents saw that detail in the commencement program and looked worried. If moving to a place (now even farther from home) where I knew no one to work behind the camera was such a great idea, why was no one else following a similar plan?

I didn't even consider telling them about my part-time status or my lowly salary. I had saved up a little more than $10,000 (holy crap—ten grand!) from my job managing the tech support team at Harvard Business School to cover the anticipated shortfall. A job, by the way, that paid $25 an hour. I was taking a massive pay cut to get into news. But, I reasoned, all I needed was a promotion to full-time reporter before the money ran out and I would be fine. Better than fine. I'd be a real live reporter.

My parents helped me move to Portland, a quaint seaside town filled with art lovers and microbrew lovers alike. They insisted I rent a one-bedroom condo built on a pier in the Old Port section of town. The unit was all sunshine and blue ocean, blue-sky beauty (and new construction), and way out of my budget. This would have been a great time to mention my teeny, tiny paycheck. But I didn't.

They went back to California, and I began my job, perfecting my skills ripping apart reams of carbon-printed scripts, so I could separate the pink, blue, and yellow copies from the carbon paper in one lightning-fast tear. Then I'd stack the papers in color-coded piles, one for the anchor, one for the producer, and one for the teleprompter operator (which was also me). I cut video to go with the stories the anchor would be reading, and more than once ran down the stairs and shoved the tape into the humming deck at the last second before we hit air, just like Joan Cusack's wonderfully accurate slapstick scene from *Broadcast News*.

Even though normal digital prompters had already existed for years, this NBC outpost was so low-budget, they still had the kind that required the teleprompter operator to lay the pages in order on a conveyor belt, while a camera lens recorded the image and projected the words onto the screen in front of the anchors. The problem came when the order of the stories had to suddenly change, because a tape or a reporter wasn't ready, or a live truck lost the signal back to the station. I was supposed to rearrange the papers fast as lightning, while the producer yelled the new order into my headset. Inevitably, I would fumble with the scripts while the anchor fumed, with the mounting pressure causing my hands to shake and making my fingers even less responsive to orders being shouted in my ears between expletives. When we finally hit a commercial break, the anchor would rip me a new one.

Other than that though, I was in heaven!

At least for a short while.

Fast forward six months: I was still ripping scripts and running the prompter for minimum wage, and the news director seemed to have forgotten his promise that this job was a very temporary foot in the door to bigger and better things. I'd made a slew of fun friends among the other young kids trying to get their start like me, but I was running out of both cash and patience. I knew I couldn't stay on in Portland forever, no matter how good I'd gotten at running prompter, so I started calling news directors in other New England towns to tell them I was "going to be in their area meeting with the competition" again.

⊶⊷

Jack Heath, the news director at WMUR in Manchester, New Hampshire, bravely gave me the break I was desperate for. The sun shines on Manchester once every four years, when every would-be president descends on the state to court voters. They say that each New Hampshire resident expects to meet a candidate three times before considering voting for them. Can you imagine meeting any candidate once, much less three times, and each one of them at that? Sounds exhausting. And tedious. But not to "First in the Nation" New Hampshire. Primary season is their time to take center stage.

But primary season doesn't last forever. For a few weeks, the world hangs on the considered political opinion of every Joe the Plumber buying coffee at the local diner, and then, almost as suddenly, the world looks away and forgets where to find the pizza-slice-shaped state on the map (is that Vermont?). The reporters, crews, news vans, and political tourists vanish without a trace. As if they were never there. The circus moves on to South Carolina, and New Hampshire goes back to being a simple, sparsely populated stretch of mostly frigid land. They call New Hampshire the granite state for a reason. When the satellite trucks clear, it's mostly just granite.

I met Jack Heath one political season when every journalist in the region was fighting over the last marginally clean, wildly overpriced motel room, a few days ahead of New Hampshire's vote. A fledgling cable channel was struggling to get off the ground. And to get a jump on its political reporting, the outfit calling itself Fox News Channel wooed away Carl Cameron, WMUR's biggest political insider. Carl knew every political operative and, I'm betting, every operative's darkest secret. He had a Rolodex that could make a would-be freshman senator weep.

His departure, though glorious, left a gaping hole in WMUR's lineup, and an opening on the payroll. That's where Jack found a spot for me, though I would replace Carl in pure headcount terms only. There was no way a twenty-two-year-old cub reporter could do justice to the legend that was Carl Cameron.

I was so green at the job I would surely glow. Anyone could see that.

But Jack reassured me I didn't need to fill Carl's enormous shoes (in addition to being a reporting legend, he's also roughly ten feet tall). Just tread in the path he'd cleared. I'd be up to speed in no time, and my political-economic background at Harvard would give me a base of knowledge and some common sense while I worked out the kinks in my on-air performance.

"No worries," he said, in offering me the job. "It's all about attitude and energy. You've got the raw material. You're like filet mignon, with the Harvard degree and all that. We'll teach you the ropes."

I was certain he meant the raw-meat reference in the nicest, most appropriate possible way.

There was a tragic flaw in Jack's plan, however. He was under the very mistaken impression that my career in television acting had somehow prepared me for television news reporting, at least a little bit. Nothing could have been further from the truth. In fact, my experience was more of a handicap than anything else. I came from a world where we rehearsed every scene until we all wanted to cry from the repetition. Writers, producers, costume designers, and makeup artists scrutinized every detail of the run through to the point of psychosis, before we put the whole dance on film. Then God forbid I flubbed a line, the director would yell "Cut!" . . . and we could head back to our opening spots and try the whole dance again.

News is quite the opposite. When you see a local reporter in the field, she's flying without a net. There's no rehearsal, no one writing the lines, no one fixing her hair or applying her make-up. No one making sure everything is just right. That's why there are so many delightfully humiliating reporter outtakes on You-Tube. We've all had the stranger stop by to potentially pants us, or the bird fly by to use our polyester jacket for target practice, all on live television.

The noon show was just starting that day, with both anchors chirping out the morning's headlines. All the people Jack hired were New England gorgeous. That preppy, just-finished-rowing, where-are-my-twin-chocolate-labs-Astor-and-Archibald?, could-my-teeth-be-any-more-sparkly? type of gorgeous. I couldn't see the anchor who had tossed to me because in the field there's only the black hole of the camera lens in front of you. But in the silence that had elapsed since the anchor's introduction, I could feel his perfectly groomed eyebrows rising ever so slightly on his un-blemished forehead (obviously this was pre-Botox—no one's eyebrows move anywhere any more).

I can't remember if I actually said any human words. I think my lips moved, but I can't be certain. If I had to bet, I would say I'd sounded like Charlie Brown's immortal "wah-wah-wah-wah-WAH-wah!" teacher.

Thank God Al Gore had not invented the Internet yet, because this world-class humiliation would have been Auto-Tuned and shared more aggressively than an Anthony Wiener wiener photo.

Jack had sent Jim Breen, WMUR's most seasoned photographer, on location with me to "help." (Great job, Jim!) Jim came out from behind the camera the second the control room cleared us.

"Sit down," he said, in a helpful/terrified tone. "Just sit down, right where you are. Sit right on the ground if you have to."

Apparently I was going to faint, and Jim didn't want me to crack my head on the State House steps.

On the ride back, I stared out the window at the harsh landscape of my defeat.

"Do you think anyone was watching?" I ventured, hoping Jim would throw me a bone.

"Well, our whole building was watching, you can count on that," he chuckled (thanks again, Jim). "You're the new girl. They want to see what you're made of."

Crikey.

Over the next few months, I got very marginally better. My nerves were killing me. The worse I was, the worse I got. I couldn't get out of my own way.

Finally, our shiny-haired, sparkly-toothed anchor Mike Beaudet shared a simple secret. "Try just talking," he coached, as if I were a complete moron. "Pretend like you're telling the story to a friend. It doesn't have to be perfect. You're just trying too hard. Relax. Tell the story like we're at a bar. Or lunch. You're fun and funny around the newsroom. But that goes away when I toss to you on camera. Like, way far away. You have to just talk to people. Or just talk to me."

Shazam! That was it! Mike had shared a smidge of the secret sauce. I got leaps and bounds better. I was still horrible, but this was still a very small market, so if the lead actor in the eighth-grade musical passed for awesome, I was now like the hearing impaired girl they let sing way too loudly in the chorus.

Sadly for me, the bolt of helpful lightning came too late.

Jack, always a political animal, decided to throw his hat in the ring for the First District congressional seat, which was suddenly vacated. That's reaching for the stars, New Hampshire style.

My lone cheerleader left me with these parting words: "You'll be great, kid. Don't worry."

To which I thought: Holy Christ, I'm screwed.

--=•=--

In their infinite wisdom, the station managers promoted the main female anchor to fill Jack's spot as news director. I'm not saying this is what happened, but if you want to ease a very capable woman whose only flaw is packing a little too much carry-on in the under-eye bag department off the air, and replace her with someone young enough to be her daughter, give the older woman a promotion, and she probably won't even notice what's just happened, right? I mean, that's a totally original move that no one has ever tried before so who would smoke that out? Of course that's not what they did. But to the naked, highly suspicious, not completely blind eye, that's a tiny bit what this move looked like.

And as her first order of business at eight o'clock on her first morning as news director, my new boss, Kristen, invited me into her office and ominously closed the door. I sat down across from her with a big, fat smile on my face. She'd shared makeup tips with me in the bathroom before her show several times. I thought this would be more womanly advice. I brought a pad and pencil to prove my complete and total ignorance of how the world works and what was about to kick me in the face harder than a mule's hind leg.

"I'm so sorry to do this," she said, very matter of fact. "But I have to let you go. You just aren't ready to be a reporter here."

I looked behind me to see who she could possibly be talking to.

"What?" Clearly I'd misheard her. Or I'd walked into an early test run for Ashton Kutcher's *Punk'd*.

"You're just too young," she explained, like that made all the sense in the world. "It's not your fault. It's Jack's, really. He never should have hired you." She shook her head like "That silly Jack! Always hiring people who need to be immediately fired! What a prankster!"

Tears started pouring down my face and bouncing into my lap. The sudden waterworks did nothing to slow down Kristen's parade of logic as to why I so obviously needed to be taken into the street and shot, just so that no one would ever be forced to watch me on television again.

"It wasn't fair to you. Or to the station. After all, this is the number four market in the country," she boasted.

Number four market? No one took that seriously. New Hampshire was such a minuscule television market at the time, that if you counted up every black and white or color set with duct-taped rabbit ears in every home, in every town, in every corner of the state, the whole enchilada didn't add up to enough to qualify as a standalone entity, so the Nielsen Ratings gurus lumped the city in with Boston, the nearest market that registered on their radar. No one else in their right mind considered Manchester part of the Boston market, certainly not the advertisers buying commercial time.

"But I'm working so hard!" I protested through tears and snot.

She sat back in her chair with her hands folded neatly in her lap. Her thin brown bob was tucked behind her ears. Then Kristen leaned forward just slightly and pushed the box of Kleenex I hadn't noticed a millimeter closer to me. Such a gesture of warmth and compassion.

I grabbed a tissue and smeared the makeup around my eyes, trying to dab away my embarrassment. She sighed at my display.

"I know you're trying . . . but just not here," she said, as if I were a poodle trying to do my business in front of her house. "Somewhere smaller."

That could only mean an affiliate in Antarctica.

I continued begging and pleading. This was perhaps my worst moment. Maybe ever. I did everything shy of offering her cash. And she didn't soften one degree.

When she'd had enough of my sad, pathetic display, she informed me that I had thirty minutes to gather my things and turn in my badge.

Thirty minutes! To take my career and shove it. Not even an hour.

Thirty.

Minutes.

"If you really need to, you could come back at a later time, with my permission and proper supervision, and dub the material you might need to look for another job."

With that, she stood up and smoothed her skirt, to make sure she hadn't become wrinkled in the exchange. My signal to get out.

The neck of my blouse was soaked through by the shower of uncontrolled tears that I had shed in the past few minutes. I could only imagine what my face looked like. My cheeks burned with a salty mix of humiliation and despair.

Just then I realized that I would have to walk out of her office and through the newsroom for all my colleagues to see. There was no way to make a dignified exit.

I shuffled toward my cubicle with my eyes fixed firmly on the brown and grey carpet that swirled around my feet. When I got to my desk, right on top, I found a sad, empty box already waiting for me. Empty. Left by someone who knew I was getting fired long before I did.

The next thing I knew, I was pushing through the door of my apartment and collapsing on the carpet in a heap of wailing cries. I let my tears sink into the rug. My bag of tricks felt empty.

That went on for a while.

Then a bit longer.

Eventually . . . I ran out of tears. Quite literally. So I got a carton of chocolate chip ice cream out of the freezer, and a fork to scrape out the stubborn bits of chocolate on the bottom, and sat on the couch to consider my options.

I really didn't have any.

What was I going to do? Move back to California? Return to my childhood home a total and complete failure? Not likely. Go back to Maine and ask for my old job back, ripping scripts and getting screamed at while I ran prompter? I was more likely to wander into traffic than to do that.

The way I saw the situation, I had two options. I could lie down on the floor of my apartment and die (which seemed tempting, I won't lie). Or I could scrape myself up off the ground and fight my way back. I didn't see very many other choices.

I needed to get back on television. But how? It's pretty hard to find a job when you don't have one. Especially if you've been fired. Everyone who's been there knows that. You carry the putrid stink of termination with you everywhere you go.

I called Jack and told him the whole sad story, since it was entirely his fault.

"I'm sorry," he offered (gee, thanks Jack!). "But you know what? There's not much you can do except get out there and prove her wrong. Come on, kid. You've been on television your whole life. You can do this. You just gotta convince someone else to put you on the air the way you convinced me. You've got all the raw ingredients. You just need a little practice. Attitude and energy. You'll get there. Let me know what I can do to help."

No meat analogy this time? That's a shame.

But in this nuclear disaster, I would learn the most essential lesson of life:

The Formula for Turning Undeniable Disaster into a Golden Opportunity

I put this guaranteed winning formula into step-by-step instructions just in case you are too broken up by my Kristen-Fired-Me-Story to really focus.

Step #1: Wallow in a bubbling vat of self-pity.

Like me blubbering on the floor of my apartment, wailing, "God why me? What did I do to deserve such scorn? Why have you abandoned me in this granite wasteland?"

I know that sounds self-indulgent. Pitiful in fact. But that's the point. If you don't dive into the grief headfirst and really feel sorry for yourself, you deny the misery. And the pain festers. And lingers like the horrible smell that clings to the microwave when some idiot at your office heats up last night's garlic-infused cod, with no thought of the fact that he's making everyone around him feel the urge to vomit.

My mother used to say, "Really cry and let it all out!" Of course, it's possible she had just read a book on reverse psychology, which completely blew up in her face when I took her up on her suggestion to sob openly and loudly. Either way, I learned that when you give way to your tears with abandon, you'll find that you only have so many. And then you're cried out. And frankly a little bored. And looking around for what's next.

Step #2: Identify what could replace your loss that's actually better (I call this "sticking it to defeat"!).

That's right. I said it. Replace the loss with something better. A step up. Defeated? Aim even higher.

Yes, that sounds insane, but there's something satis-
fyingly cocky in giving failure the middle finger. Not
only did you not kill me, failure, you've made me
stronger. I am better for your evil deeds!

Even if you don't believe any of that the first time
you chant those words in the mirror, you will in time.
I promise. Add a cocktail and you're good. (But only
one, because two drinks at this moment will send you
riiiiiight back to Step #1. Just a warning.)

*Step #3: Identify the first thing you need to do to start
down the path to your goal (I call this the "get your ass in
gear" step).*

This is essential. Laying out the entire distance
you need to travel is overwhelming and fraught with
way too many variables. The mess looks too big for
any one person to clean up . . . like my sons' rooms.
And there are way too many scary unknowns. Like
my sons' room.

Don't worry about any of that (or you'll lie down
in traffic)—all you need at this moment is one step.
One measly step. One small victory to get you rolling the right direction. And out of your pajamas. Once
you have a tiny taste of recovery, continuing becomes
infinitely easier. Cake. You're on your way.

So . . . back to me.

The first thing I needed (besides a fresh carton of
chocolate chip ice cream) was a reel. I needed to piece
together any decent slices of airtime I could muster.
Yes, I had done a ton of sucking, but there were—very

few, I'll admit—glimmers of some not totally horrible moments when I had found a way to get past the
panic.

I just needed to sew those glimmers into a
three-minute stretch. Even two minutes would be
fine . . . news directors have short attention spans just
like everyone else.

Luckily, I had been saving some of my on-air
work—to watch and learn from, but also in prepara-
tion to flee the state for a bigger market as soon as
possible (no offense, New Hampshire).

Jack-whose-fault-this-was-anyway had offered up
the name of a shop that created political ads. As a favor
to him the ad dudes volunteered to work their magic
putting together my sorry little clips of semi-startled
news reporting and then make a few copies. What an
enormous relief! I wouldn't need to crawl back to my
former boss to use her equipment under the watchful
eye of her Soviet-style security detail.

After that—you guessed it!—I picked up my '90s-
era cordless phone that charged on an enormous base
and began dialing up news directors to let them know
that I was coming to town to interview with the competition. Yes, I dusted off that old trick, and what do
you know? It still worked.

What was one step better than the job I'd lost in
a sorry display of snot and tears? Well, if you believed
my former boss, there were only three bigger television markets on the planet, but no noninsane person

believed that garbage. That was just kooky talk. I
knew enough to realize there were probably fifty or
sixty markets in the eastern half of the country further up the food chain than Manchester.

So I set my sights on the lovely, charming college
town of Providence, Rhode Island—home of Brown
University and Vincent "Buddy" Cianci, a mayor so
beloved that once he finished serving his time for fed-
eral racketeering, he returned home, not to the mayor's
office, sadly, but to be celebrated with his own weekly
television show (less lucrative than public corruption
but almost as good). What a colorful place to work as
a local reporter!

I could see no downside to picking up the phone
and trying to drum up a few meetings, starting in
Providence; then I'd fan out from there.

Wah-lah! Look at me! Put a big black check mark
next to steps 2 and 3. Go me! Hooray! I'd put a bull's-
eye on my replacement (better) job and taken the first
step toward digging my way out of this giant, awful
mess.

During the next few months, I drove around New England, and even boarded a few Southwest flights to
Florida, in search of my next job. Many times I felt
adrift in a sea of hopelessness and wondered why I'd
even decided on this absurdly difficult career path,
so divergent from anything I knew and anything my

classmates were doing a year or two out of college (they were too smart and rational for this idiocy).

During the many hours I spent driving down the interstate from one Waffle House to the next, following the black Sharpie arrows on my AAA TripTik maps, I had time to think about what I'd learned. Which led to the final step in my self-styled formula.

Step #4: Decide what to do differently next time.

I replayed that nightmare scene in Kristen's office in my mind six thousand times (spoiler alert: I got fired every time). And one piece of dialogue really stuck out like a sore thumb, when Kristen said, "You're just too young . . ."

I was no lawyer, but I didn't think you could fire someone based on age alone. Didn't we fight a war based on that? No, that's not right. But there had been some marching somewhere based on that principle. Or a law or a guideline at least.

I knew what she meant—she thought I was too inexperienced and didn't deserve the job. But still, you wouldn't say something that left you open to reprisal like that unless you thought the person you were talking to was utterly powerless. I had no one backing me up. I needed some mob-style protection. I'd never operated this way in the past. As a child on television, I had a stage mother and an agent. That's muscle. Double muscle. I was too old for the first one, but the second one, I could certainly use. So I made a vow to myself that the next time I sat down across the desk from someone in a position to fire me, I'd have an agent to back me up. I hired the guy behind some of the best-known talent in network news at the time to let the world know I meant business.

The search took all summer, but by the fall I had landed a job in Providence, Rhode Island.

Woot! Woot! Go me! It's my birthday! Go shorty! It's my birthday!

Then more celebrating. (There were some tequila shots at this juncture that ultimately resulted in my wedding. But that's a story for another time and another chapter.)

As I rolled into Providence, set up my third apartment in less than two years, and prepared for my first day back on the air, I told the butterflies in my stomach the personal truth I had just learned: you just can't kill me. At least, not without a very serious weapon. If you knock me down, I'm going to get back up. If you shoot me in the leg, I'm going to put a Band-Aid on the bullet hole and keep right on going. And then I'm going to stick it to the shooter by marching past my original goal and onto something better. (And yes, I will eventually find time to get the bullet extracted so I'm not killed by a raging infection later, which would be ironic . . . don't focus on that part, you get my point.)

Watch out, world.

⤛⊷⊙ ⊙⊶⤜

I've heard people say that getting fired was the best thing that ever happened to them. I'd always thought those people (1) were completely stupid, (2) were completely annoying, or (3) read that ridiculous slogan in a fortune cookie but were never actually fired themselves and only pretending because they thought they sounded cool.

In other words, I didn't buy that cheap line, mainly because I'd already lived an entire career, an entire life, as a professional actor in Hollywood. As an actor, you get "fired" every time a shoot ends. You go from being gainfully employed as the center of attention in front of the lens, with people fussing over you and bringing you free food, to collecting unemployment with no idea when or if you'll ever work again. And that's not even accounting for the rejection that taunts you every time you don't get past the first audition. That uncertainty sucked, each and every time. In that sense, I'd been fired a zillion times, and there was nothing redeeming about the experience.

When I lost the job in New Hampshire, the blow knocked the wind right out of me. Here I thought I'd found a more certain career, and I couldn't believe I was being forced to rebuild yet again. But now I was back, baby! And I'd proven to myself I could get up from any defeat.

And I would need that strength the next time life sent me flying off a cliff, Wile E. Coyote style.

That next thermonuclear meltdown was a long time in coming. Seven years after I left Manchester, my husband (the one I acquired during the tequila celebration . . . by the way, I'm not totally certain I'm going to end up telling you that story because I don't come off so great and my dad is probably reading this book). Anyhow, Wray and I had moved out to San Francisco just in time for the tech bubble to burst. They say timing is everything in life.

We got to spend a little less than two years enjoying our carefree Bay Area lifestyle, tooling around our Marina neighborhood in our silver-blue convertible, but by July 4, 2002, I was getting the distinct sense that my days at CNET, the tech news company, were numbered.

CNET had built an enormous, shiny new headquarters building, which is always the most certain kiss of death, like the grinning athlete who lands on the cover of *Sports Illustrated* only to completely choke before the magazine even leaves the newsstand (in tech bubble terms, think Pets.com blowing a huge wad of cash on a Super Bowl ad, of all stupid things, then promptly going belly up).

Shortly after we cut the comically large yellow bow on the front door and moved into our shiny new cubicles, management was forced to shutter many of the vanity businesses that weren't contributing to revenue in order to focus on the core website. As a result, they were cutting the television unit—my unit—to the bone.

Wray and I watched the Independence Day fireworks with friends that year, and walked back to the adorable pink-hued home on the waterfront we'd just bought (also a kiss of death move). Our first house with a yard.

The noise of the fireworks bursting in air drowned out the ringing of my cell phone, signaling another tragedy. Repeated calls had come from my father, who was trying to tell me my sister had suddenly died. While he sat bawling helplessly as paramedics tended to my sister, crumpled up on the floor of their southern California home just five hours away, Wray and I had been sitting hand in hand, quietly celebrating the holiday and imagining the rest of our lives together. (Sorry, this is not a jokey moment.)

Now, I've written a whole book about my life as the daughter of a stage mother, and the high-pressured air of craziness and uncertainty that engulfed our shared childhoods. Surviving the fumes made me a fighter and gave me the strength I would need later to face people like that news director in New Hampshire, but the same environment choked my sister, Tiffany, with self-loathing and doubt. With her spirit destroyed by my mother's unceasing disappointment, she'd escaped for years with alcohol. What made her death even harder to accept was that she'd been on the mend, sober for a while, living with my dad, who had given up everything in his life to devote himself to her recovery. And to my mind, he was finally, finally winning the long fight to help her.

When he got through to me on that Fourth of July night with the shocking news that Tiffany's body had simply given up, I was knocked to the ground, flattened, crushed. This was no firing. With Tiffany's death, a piece of our souls had been snuffed out, and I knew even in those first dark moments that the pain of a loss like this would never leave me but would instead simply morph from a blinding, burning, knife-like wound to a dull ache that constantly nags, like a reminder of an amputated limb.

A few days after my sister died, as I returned to San Francisco from helping my dad to deal with the horrific details of Tiffany's death, my boss at CNET told me through her own sheet of tears that she was laying me off. The news hurt her far worse than me. She couldn't bear to take away the job of a person who'd just lost her only sibling, but she had no choice. I was already so hobbled by shock that I barely noticed this incremental step further down into the pit of despair and loss.

In fact, I had lost so much in the space of a few days I was afraid to cross the street or leave the house once I returned home with my box of belonging from my desk. I believed, with reason, that the universe was hunting me down for specific punishment. Seemed logical. I still had Wray. That was a lot. And my health, I guess, though every breath I took made me feel guilty I had oxygen and Tiffany did not. But crossing the street seemed like a gamble with fate I'd certainly lose. Ditto for stepping outside if there was lightning anywhere in the vicinity.

In that frozen state I went back to those handy steps I'd jazzed up in Manch-Vegas New Hampshire.

First, I locked the door to our home. Even to friends. I hid inside. Pulled the shades. Sat mostly on the floor. Didn't answer the phone. Got furious and cursed God. Then I watched *NYPD Blue* reruns—or, at least, put them on the television while I lay on the couch and stared at the screen. They also sold chocolate chip ice cream in California, much like New Hampshire, so I got a few big tubs and a fork (a fork works better on the chips. You're welcome.).

Step #1: Wallow in a huge bubbling vat of self-pity. Check.

Next, I had to identify what would be better. I couldn't replace my only sister. That was clear. But I could find a new job. I'd loved CNET, but I was only working there because Wray's job in finance had brought us out west. The real job I'd wanted, my dream job, was reporting financial news for CNBC. Back in the business school lounge when I wasn't fixing computers, I'd watched Maria Bartiromo rocket to fame as the "Money Honey," the first brilliant and beautiful face to report live from the floor of the New York Stock Exchange. The genius of that nickname says it all. She was wicked smart and rocking the sexy, gorgeous Sophia Loren vibe at the same time. Who wouldn't want to be her? She was all that and a bag of chips, and still is.

I'd passed up an offer to report for a magazine show on CNBC before coming out to California with Wray. Now I wondered if that had been such a wise choice. I decided that making good on my dream to work at CNBC would begin to fill the gaping chasm that the last week had created. I would take a stab at replacing my job with a better one. That much I might be able to do.

Step #2: Identify what could replace your loss that's actually better. (Middle finger to disaster.) Check.

I got my agent cracking on Project CNBC. (*Step #3: Take the first step to achieving your goal.*) I was getting my rear in gear. And within a month or so, amazingly, we'd secured an offer. Wray and I were heading back to New York. I was on the road to recovery and waving at misery in the rearview. But now I had to Scotch-tape my heart back together and figure out how to sidestep the next crisis that would track me down like a P.I. getting the goods on a wayward spouse.

(*Step #4: Decide what to do differently.*)

So what had I learned from this disaster? (Beside the fact that Andy Sipowitz always always always played the bad cop about to blow his gasket in the interrogations room of *NYPD Blue*. How dumb were those criminals?)

What would I do differently now? That would take a lot of time in therapy to sort through. Like every other person who has ever walked the face of the Earth (and probably most aliens in outer space), I had an emotionally rough childhood that I carried around everywhere. *Wahhhhhhh! Poor me! Poor you! Poor everyone!* We could all write a book, play, or really emotional Adele song about our own particular scars. We could sit paralyzed by whatever happened to us and feel really bad for ourselves and never get married/have kids/leave the house. I was hardly unique in my struggles.

The universal nature of tough childhoods aside, I realized at this point that Wray and I had been married for a while and I wasn't going to have the stomach to have children of my own until I sorted through my garbage and decided what to keep, recycle, and just plain throw away.

Holy cow that was a long, painful process.

Now brace yourself: I'm going to throw a little religion at you here. (There's actually a bunch of God coming in a later chapter, and if that makes you uncomfortable, feel free to skip that chapter entirely. You won't hurt my feelings—I'm totally cool with that.)

"The worst is never the last," the theologian Frederick Buechner said. He was talking about the resurrection of Christ. I can imagine when Jesus was crucified, the Apostles were like, "Well, this is the worst possible outcome. I did not see this coming. I actually liked Judas. Things could not get worse." And they were right. They'd lived to see the guy they thought was the be-all, end-all get nailed to wood and die a horrific, painful, humiliating death. Then they'd fled for their lives. Whatever we've been through, I can't imagine topping that in terms of pure suffering and terror. I hope I can't ever top that. But then the resurrection came along and an entire religion was born and everyone who wanted to could wipe the slate clean and have a new life.

The worst was not the last. Luckily, and thank God, it never is. You just have to find a way (use my steps!) and the strength to dig deep and move on.

Chapter Two

Nice Guys (and Gals) Finish First

The first time I rolled around in the mud with Allison Balson, I felt utterly ridiculous. I've never been the type of girl to raise my fists. That on-camera fight would be the first of many dustups in which my character would clash with hers.

When we read through the scene initially, my mother explained to me that this girl, who was a little taller and older than I, was coming to the show to reignite the drama that the Laura/Nellie struggle had added to the *Little House* storylines. In other words, they were once again combing through the filing cabinets for old scripts and putting them back to work.

When I met Allison, she politely introduced herself.

"Hello," she smiled, revealing huge white teeth, ten shades lighter than her white blonde locks. So this would be Cassandra's nemesis, I thought. I could see our characters' connection, our symmetry and contrast, stretching out before us, like a tree and its shadow.

That villain and hero formula is easy to write but tougher to swallow. In real life, I wasn't totally convinced the Good Guy won in the end. I'd seen other kids get away with murder, like when the teacher arrived too late to know who'd started the hair pulling. I could think of more than a few times both my sister and I were sent to our rooms, though only one of us deserved the punishment. Luckily, there was a pro on hand to eclipse my skepticism. No one knew the power of positivity better than Michael Landon. I never met anyone who worked for him who wouldn't say, "He's good to people! What a great guy! He cares about his crew." Perhaps there were people in his personal life who would quibble with this assessment, but that's not my business.

He was like a perfect kindergarten teacher who makes all the kids believe they are the special favorite, but inspires just enough fear to keep even the worst children from eating all the crayons before lunch. Not very many bosses operate this effectively. Anyone who witnessed the *Little House* team would agree: that set just hummed.

Every once in a while I will flip past the Hallmark Channel and pause on a few minutes of the show, trying to see if things were really as I remembered them. The last time this happened, the Ingalls were celebrating Christmas (people still called it Christmas way back then) when a blizzard decided to crush Walnut Grove. Instead of calling in the National Guard (there wasn't one), this cheery group decided to sit around the fire and remember Christmas Gone By.

Okay, here's the truth: Michael figured out that a totally brilliant way to save some dough on production was to reuse clips of old episodes as heart-warming memories and string them together with some narration. And . . . presto! You've got a fresh episode on the cheapity cheap! No wonder he had an epic mansion in Malibu!

While the snow stacked up inch by inch, the extended family warmed themselves with tales of holidays gone by (or pressed rewind on all the previous seasons). Then the adults fell asleep, sitting up at ninety-degree angles in their hard-as-rock chairs around the small, splintery wooden table, and the kids slept soundly in the loft, six to a bed.

In the morning, the Ingalls children, including me, awoke to the absence of presents. The horror! Charles reassured the kids that the deep snow held Santa's advance at the barn, which he could quickly remedy by braving the white powder and fetching the gifts himself. But when he heaved opened the front door, a solid wall of snow blocked every inch of light. (In reality, on the Culver City set, the set decorators had stapled a sheet of white foam insulation over the door to block us in. What looked like ice was really thick, itchy fabric—but such were the magical powers of our special effects department, circa 1980.)

Certainly, a blizzard that nearly crushed our tiny home of sticks and threatened to suffocate us wouldn't slow down Charles. Pa scrambled up the ladder to the kids' loft and chuckled while asking Ma for his snow shoes. His plan? To walk on frozen water to the barn and fetch the gifts—not terribly subtle, from a biblical perspective.

After saving Christmas on film, Michael yelled cut and did nearly the same thing in the flesh. Every year he gave each and every member of the cast and crew a rockin' gift that blew our minds. My mother told me he didn't pick up the huge tab for the over-the-top extravagance; he built a clause into his network contract obligating NBC Productions to underwrite the whole scene—more financial genius. But he picked the gift and dealt the boxes, playing Santa just the same.

The year we shot Recycled Christmas, Michael handed out a hundred of these new fangled whiz-bangs called a video tape recorder. Beta decks! "I remember the great battle of Beta versus VHS!" says no one reading this book. All you need to know is that everyone at this period of time watched shows only at the precise time they aired on television . . . and had to sit through commercials (my kids just screamed in horror). These were the dark ages, and this gift was like giving each of us our own self-driving car (my kids just screamed with delight).

The silver machine was the size and weight of a six-year-old child. The slot for the tape popped up from the body of the contraption like the escape pod of a flying saucer. We couldn't believe our eyes.

Michael had the prop truck backed up to the stage door, where cardboard boxes containing the loot spilled out of the truck and into the waiting hands of the frenzied staff. Everyone got the exact same gift, whether hair stylists, the cinematographer, stand-ins, or the show's biggest female star, Melissa Gilbert.

Michael's message was crystal clear: you are all equally important to me. All of your contributions are essential. Monday nights at eight o'clock on NBC wouldn't happen without YOU. Thank you.

And Merry Christmas from Santa/God/Me.

If the actors thought we were better than the key grip or the best boy because we stood in front of the camera and the others stood way, way behind the lens, we could guess again. Christmas was the day Michael showed us we were a team of equals.

Of course, even at the age of eight, I was keenly aware that our weekly paychecks were not equal. The way my mother's chest swelled when that envelope arrived in the mailbox told me that much. But this was a very public way for Michael to acknowledge us as a workforce of equals, at least on this day.

Michael was a man's man when that was thought to be a good thing. A Macho Macho Man. He loved to hang out with the rough and tumble crew, ragged around the edges, spitting on the ground—outside his beautiful sound stage, not in it, thank you. He respected what they did, and they ate up the fact he preferred them to hoity-toity actors, rolling up their sleeves to see who could produce more sweat alongside their extra-cool king.

I don't think this was so much his clever strategy to squeeze the maximum work out of every employee as it was his personality. But the way he ran his team paid huge dividends. I was certainly standing in the corner quietly taking notes. I'd already been on a lot of sets, and this one ran a hell of a lot faster and more efficiently than the others. We jammed in more scenes before lunch than others did all day. I know because of the number of lines I had to memorize at night to be ready for the next day.

Michael's example made it clear: you're not just a revolting human being if you don't respect the people around you and treat them well; you're also a moron because you desperately need these men and women to get their jobs done on time and under budget. I'm still shocked by the number of people who don't do this math.

Now in my new TV life, I have seen way too many psycho-diva anchors abuse and berate a young producer or a tech op. And then, shocker of shockers! The prompter stops working, or a script accidentally disappears. But perhaps the most idiotic is the suicidal talent who abuses the hair and makeup team. Talk about people who have power to literally make you look wretched! I've seen women grab makeup brushes from artists and show them how to do their job, or rip hair brushes or curling irons from stylists' hands to correct their technique. Mind you, these artists own these tools. I remember one woman in particular who was famous for this type of degrading behavior. One day I saw her on air, ghost-white complexion with gothic lips and Groucho Marx brows. I knew she had pissed off the wrong artist.

The implication is so clear. When you abuse people around you for sport, they will take their revenge (and roar with laughter). Plus, you are going to make your own mistakes and need help from these very same people. THEY WILL NOT HELP YOU IF YOU'VE ABUSED THEM. Duh!

Another important fact: when you are being evil to the people around you, you end up with a headache from all the stress and fighting. Work isn't very fun. The day becomes one long battle. Though the greatest sin by far in this is the fact you are crushing a lot of feelings under the spikey heel of your boot.

If you have a good attitude and incorporate a laugh or two, who knows? You might actually have fun at work. You might accidentally like your coworkers and enjoy your job! And of course there's the bonus of qualifying as a decent human being.

There's this woman who works in the little food joint in our building. Her name is Ocean, and she always has a huge smile on her face and a cheerful greeting for everyone who comes in. She asks about your kids and laughs about how much she loves hers. And gets the line moving so fast you feel as if you're already knocked up with caffeine, which is the whole point of the stop. And you come away thinking Ocean must be grateful not just to have a job but to be alive.

But that's not to say that everywhere you look, the Good Guys or Gals are leading the charge and winning the race. I firmly believe they do finish the race at the front, but Lord knows Evil Doers can lead for long stretches that make me want to rip my hair out of my head. Long before I came to Fox, I worked with a woman who, if you believed the rather loud gossip, got ahead the old-fashioned way—not a technique ever featured on *Little House on the Prairie* (though when we were trying to boost ratings this could have been another way to go). This woman's supposed way of currying favor with male bosses would have fit more neatly on Cinemax After Dark.

I have no proof of what really happened. Unless I've seen someone commit a crime with my own eyes, I cannot judge them guilty. But guilty or not, this woman had a habit of coming and going from a shop in blink of an eye, always with a tellingly brief tenure. After she'd disappeared from our shop, one of my bosses, who had previously backed her, was talking about what terrible talent she was. Turns out he had noticed that she couldn't conduct an interview without

reading her questions from a teleprompter and strug-
gled to respond to developing news around her. What
a sudden change in tune! I asked him why she'd lasted
as long as she did, even though, as he finally admitted,
she wasn't up to the job.

"To be honest, I wanted a . . . " (I can't write the
word, my children are reading over my shoulder. But it
sounds like nose job.)

Wow.

I thanked my boss for his honesty. At least this
chapter of my life finally made sense. I have to confess
my naïveté. I had no idea so many managers were still
living in a warped time when they thought they could
use their power to sort and degrade lives around them.
Whether or not this woman really traded such favors
for opportunity, talk of such payoffs were enough to
whet the appetite of future bosses who would hire
her, filled with hope. And while this woman invari-
ably piqued the interest of new managers who brought
her into their organizations, creating fanfare when she
arrived, without the news chops to back her up, she
didn't last.

I won't offer a moral—I'll let you write your own.
But that boss's comment about his base motivations
reminded me of the time I was working in a very small
market and one of the local news chiefs showed up
on my doorstep after midnight. He was clearly inebri-
ated and similarly hopeful. Turns out, even in modern times, these ogres still exist everywhere. I didn't

let this man over the threshold of my tiny apartment, and before the scene turned ugly, his mobile phone rang, drowning out his mumblings and fumblings. He looked at the incoming number and said, "Christ! It's my wife. I'd like to tell her to stop driving me nuts! I'd like to tell her I'm with a smokin' twenty-four-year-old . . ."

He got quite a bit more colorful after that, including details of what he quite mistakenly thought was coming next.

I pretended I was dying (of something excruciatingly painful and highly contagious). I was willing to barf right on him to keep him from forcing his way in, and I was so panicked, I think I could have achieved that goal without much effort. As he skulked away, I knew that when he sobered up, he'd be humiliated by this exchange . . . and, possibly, furious. The light of day was only going to ripen the foul odor of this alcohol-soaked mess. So I called my agent first thing in the morning and asked her to help me get the hell out of Dodge.

There had been signs—like when I asked for a Friday off because I was going to Vegas for the weekend with friends, including my boyfriend (now husband). His response: "Don't you dare come back married or you're fired." He paused long enough before he said he was kidding for me to know that, for sure, he was not kidding.

As I loaded up my boxes and broke my lease, I asked myself what I could have possibly done to make this man think I would let him in that door? Maybe he thought my young age and obvious career ambition would cancel out my judgment? Or, even worse, that I would consider this a fair trade?

As I look back on this now, I know I should have done something much braver than pack up and leave town. I let a pig chase me from a job I'd fought for. But I thought that's how the world worked. I didn't have a long track record of good reporting work to fall back on. At twenty-four, I was struggling to break into news, to reinvent myself in a new career. I wondered if perhaps that was the reason he'd hired me. Not because he thought I might have talent, but because I might be a vulnerable target, and I needed and wanted the break so desperately. More than anything else, I didn't think anyone would care the smallest bit about a drunk man showing up on my doorstep saying vulgar things. I should have stood up for what was right, instead of protecting my own best interest. I wasn't thinking about the group, the larger good; instead I just bolted.

What I did, bolting out of town, wasn't right, and the wisdom of age and many events since have taught me that I almost certainly wasn't his first or last target. I enabled his unacceptable behavior by not calling him out. That's one of the many reasons these monsters grow bolder. I know that now. I helped the Bad Guy in this particular race keep going.

Years later I got an email from a friend who said he'd crossed paths with this Neanderthal. The friend wanted to pass along a greeting from my old boss, who said he had been watching me ascend the news ladder. The offending manager was now working in a much smaller market, and he was divorced. Isn't it interesting that he thought that his marital status was a relevant detail to be shared?

I know you're wondering, in light of these experiences, if I knew what was apparently happening around me at Fox News in the era of Roger Ailes. Like so many of my colleagues I was gob smacked by the headlines when so many of my coworkers stepped forward and accused him of demanding sexual favors in return for professional advancement. The stories didn't ring true immediately for me, though the signs were there. In spades, I now realize. But early on, like so many who came forward to defend him, that wasn't the Roger I thought I knew, and I too was ready to leap to his defense.

But as more and more people came forward, a lesson he'd shared (repeatedly) came into sharper focus. I remembered when Roger first called me to his office, shortly after I'd been hired away from CNBC. He told me he thought I had all the ingredients of his other stars.

What are those ingredients? I asked.

"A star in this business is a lot of things. She's a good friend and listener, a great mom who loves her kids, a loyal wife, but also someone with a wicked sense of humor, who can take a joke and make one, with the guys," he smiled mischievously.

"And of course," he continued, "she's someone you'd like to get into bed, and you fit that bill as far as I'm concerned, for sure," he smiled, sitting back in his chair.

"Let's hope the audience feels the same way," I said, not thinking much of the comment. Seemed like a pretty great description to me. In fact, I shared it with friends from CNBC who asked me about the genius of Roger Ailes.

He repeated the exact same description to me, at least two more times, alone in his office, using the f-word in the last part of the description. I never took the monologue as a proposition. I'd grown up in Hollywood where lots of people say lots of things, far more vulgar, as part of their dialogue, and around the edges of the studio, on the walk from the dressing rooms. I'm not shocked by banter.

I'll never know how he meant it. Even though he said nearly the exact the same thing at least three times, I simply thought he'd gotten to that point in life, with so much talent traipsing through his office, he couldn't remember which stories he'd told, when, and to whom.

But when women who had worked with him began to tell their stories, I suddenly started to wonder if I'd missed the meaning of those meetings.

Yet again I'm reminded not to let my desire to see the sunny side of life blind me to the darker underbelly that certainly exists, and the damage it can do. As I said, villains are lurking everywhere. Whether they come in the form of diva co-workers (male and female), or other people in life who track misery everywhere they go, or managers thinking with the wrong head. I could let their omnipresence dim my view of the world. But while I won't wear blinders, I also won't let the bad apples sour me to the goodness of most.

Plus, I truly do not believe those people win in the end. Their career comes to either some explosive conclusion or a painfully slow demise—I'm not sure which is worse. Their families and friends drift away from their side. As in those episodes of *Little House* that seemed so predictable, in reality, the chickens really do come home to roost. There's a reason the heavy-handed themes of light and dark, good and bad, Laura and Nellie still resonate. The contrast exists off the screen, vividly, all around us

But I refuse to stop trying every day to be a positive force.

At the age of one, my daughter Gemma developed a foolproof way to get anyone within earshot to come into her room in the morning and free her from her crib. She yells, "YEAH! YEAH! YEAH!" And claps!

Most babies cry to let the world know they need some-thing. But when you throw open her door, she grins from ear to ear, laughs, and applauds your arrival. She gives her first guest of the day a standing ovation! How could anyone possibly resist a smiling, cheering baby? I know I can't. Now her brothers, father, and I fight to be the one to get her when we hear her first peep. We fight to do exactly what she wants and needs because she rewards our attention with sunshine.

She's a positive force by nature. I won't lie to her about the world, but I won't let it trample her sweet, bright spirit either.

CHAPTER THREE

TRY NOT TO BE A LUNATIC (IF AT ALL POSSIBLE)—YOU'LL JUST DRIVE YOURSELF CRAZY

As I've mentioned, the villain of my time on *Little House* was Nancy. Nancy had it all. She'd been left for dead at an orphanage, but then by a miracle from God, she was rescued by the richest family in Walnut Grove and doted on by a mother who couldn't possibly pin enough curls on her head or kisses on her cheeks. But somehow in the face of this shockingly good fortune, Nancy still couldn't find a way to be happy. She couldn't resist the impulse to do horrible things, always biting the hand that fed her. Viewers know I mean that literally. In one of her opening episodes, she sunk her sizable teeth into Mrs. Oleson's hand in a fit of pure violence. The same hand that bought her exquisite clothes and luscious candy, finer and more luxurious than anything she'd known in her life. The same hand that plucked her from that orphanage where she was kept locked in a room like a rabid animal. Her behavior was evil and cliché in equal doses, and when she was confronted, she would hiss her signature refrain of self-pity, "You HATE me!" The Nancy Oleson character was the embodiment of a person making herself miserable for no reason. Today I'd jump back on the screen and tell her, "Hey lady. Try not to be a lunatic. Just for a day. You'll be a lot happier."

Since those days, I've met a ton of loons, and I've slipped into lunatic mode myself now and then. We all do. We allow our fear of failure, fear that someone else is getting what we want or deserve, cloud our view and push us off track, further even from our desired destination. Lunatics are people who become their own worst enemy. Stopping at the precipice of lunacy without falling over into the abyss requires (1) a completely sane understanding of what you really want in life, what would really make your heart sing, and then (2) a laser-like focus on that distinct goal, while avoiding the distraction of the lunatics around you and their antics. That's a lot to master, but the feat is worth the effort, if only to avoid turning into a stark raving crazy girl with corkscrew curls who bites.

⊷⊶⊙ ⊙⊷⊶

Thompson threw his lean little boy body on the black wood floor of our kitchen, railing against whatever cosmic unfairness I'd callously sent his way. I can't even remember what horrible thing I'd done, but clearly this grave injustice could not be tolerated. There was a principle at stake! And probably an iPad app as well! How had he been born to parents who were so intellectually and emotionally unstable? So blatantly insane?

As he wailed and cried and gnashed his teeth, I waited. And sighed. He had tremendous endurance. I had to give him that. And volume. Epic volume. World-class volume.

But the crying? Subpar at best.

I waited for a lull in the action, but clearly none was coming.

"Thompson," I said in my normal voice, which couldn't be heard above the beating of fists and chest and floor boards. "This is really horrible acting. I have to tell you."

One eye turned my way.

"I'm wondering if we are even related, frankly," I said, almost to myself.

The wails continued, but the volume dropped by 50 percent.

"I like what you're doing there," I pointed, "with the limbs flying. That's nice work. And I appreciate your heart and your commitment to this scene. The volume, as always, is spectacular. But you're missing the most essential element. Where are the real tears?"

He had both eyes on me now.

"Without real tears, like, actual liquid coming out of your eyes, without that, all the sound and fury . . . is just noise. Fake. When I was your age, I got paid real money, good money to cry, so I know what I'm talking about . . ."

The mention of cash was like a bolt of lightning to the head.

"You got paid for this?" he said in a suddenly calm voice.

"No. Not for that. No one would pay for that," I said, waving my hand at the character he'd now broken. "I got paid to cry convincingly. With real tears. Not like the other wooden children who had the makeup artist sprinkling Visine on their cheeks because they couldn't produce the real deal."

He blinked and sat up.

"What you're doing there? No one would pay for. I'm sorry. I'm don't mean to sound harsh. But it's true," I said, crossing my arms.

"How much did you make?" he asked, wanting to calculate the price per tear. He'd completely forgotten whatever had caused the tirade. This was far more important. Had much more potential.

"Quite a bit. If I told you, it'd blow your mind," I teased.

Thompson can be motivated by cash (which he hoards religiously, while spending only mine).

His performances since that day have been exponentially better. Chock full of real tears. Bravo.

I tell this story, not just because the tale is one of Megyn Kelly's favorite (she's prompted me more than once to do this bit and always snickers way too early, kind of ruining my delivery and distracting the audience). And I'm not telling it because the histrionics bear a striking resemblance to the aforementioned Nancy. But because it also illustrates one of Megyn's very best lines to live by:

Be so good they can't ignore you.

If you're going to cry, make sure you've got real tears. You've got to throw your whole self into it. Go the whole nine yards. Really commit. Be so good they can't ignore you. Now that sounds obvious. But focusing on being good, excellent even, is critical. That means not getting distracted by things like what the person next to you is getting that you're not getting, or what they have already that you don't.

Just focus on you and being the absolute best at what you're doing.

That's the first step in avoiding being a lunatic, a Nancy. Putting in the work to be excellent at what you're after.

Here's the part that stinks, that generally requires a massive amount of heavy lifting. And however hard you think you are working, you could be working harder. I learned this agonizing lesson at Harvard, where students were very used to being number one in their class and were willing to spend all night in the library, loved to exist on zero sleep, and thought nothing of having less than no social life (in fact that was a bonus to far too many).

In high school, I'd had no trouble outworking my peers. They were children, and I'd lived in the adult world, working adult hours, earning an adult pay-check, while they rode their bikes around the neigh-borhood selling the occasional Girl Scout cookie. If a teacher said to hit the books, they glanced at the pages. I memorized the book.

But when I got to Harvard, not only did every-one around me seem to have magical gifts and talents unique to each individual, they were also tireless and possessed the ability to focus and drive like a rocket blasting off for the moon, with intensity that shat-tered the sound barrier.

Entering the workforce after that was floating back down to earth gently on a lovely bed of balloons. In your average workplace, the majority of people are coasting, floating, punching their timecard. They have real distractions: a family to take care of, a mortgage, ailing parents. And less real ones: the Internet. You can beat them just by staying awake at your desk. If you focus and put the pedal to the metal, you're Em-ployee of the Week!

You can apply this principle to be good, if not great, almost anywhere, doing whatever is import-ant to you. Getting in shape, losing weight, cleaning your house, making the front yard gorgeous, or getting trained in a new field because you were replaced by a robot at your last job.

To be clear, this doesn't mean you must stay up all night working like my rather nerdy college classmates. Not at all, and in fact this is where not being a lunatic comes in handy. The secret is *economy of effort*: not spinning your wheels on crap that doesn't matter and focusing your effort on one, solitary goal at a time. Ask yourself, *What's my real goal?* Then focus on just that. And don't let your mind wander.

We all have days when it's all we can do to simply return a phone call because we're distracted and unfocussed and frankly all over the place, too busy thinking about the dinner we haven't cooked yet or even shopped for at the market. We're thinking about the other mother at preschool who droned on and on about how her daughter, Wildflower, had broken new ground in computer coding and mastered her fifth language over the summer. Or we are letting our minds wander to how ripped the gardener looked when he was shaping the bushes with those long, hard clipping sheers the day before. Boom, we're distracted and derailed.

The Ingalls weren't susceptible to distraction because distraction could be deadly. One thing that Charles did a number of times in both the books and on the television show was trade a day or two of body-breaking labor for a basic necessity, like a milking cow, or a hand in return, doing some bit of lifting and dragging on his own property. One time he helped another pioneer drive a herd of cattle past his property. This involved serving as a goalie, blocking one side of the path as a few thousand pounds of cow flew at him on thundering, rock-hard hooves. One wrong move, and Pa instantly became a piece of prairie. You bet your rear Charles stayed focused that day.

My husband, Wray, is amazingly focused, but he came to that strength in a roundabout way. What to the naked eye looks like patience and perseverance in the tireless pursuit of a single goal could also be viewed as being (forgive me, my love) a touch stubborn. (So is his mother. Do not tell her I said that.) When Wray believes in something he stays the course with his eyes locked on the finish line. I mentioned recently to him that I was hip to the fact that his dug-in quality was masquerading as a much more revered calm focus to the outside world. He smiled, amused that I'd finally reached such an obvious conclusion. Then he said, "I realized maybe a decade ago, in business negotiations, sometimes the difference between stubborn and patient is simply tone."

Genius.

For those of us with less donkey in our DNA, distractions are everywhere. Take, for example, everything on your smart phone, Facebook, even Taylor

Swift's latest breakup. Or that mom and her genetically superior wonder-daughter, Wildflower. We all know other moms like her with totally superior children like Wildflower. Is it Wildflower? Snapdragon? Carnation? Banana? I'm pretty sure the kid's name is Banana.

When Annoying Mom tortures you at drop-off for the fifty-fifth time about the latest language that Banana has mastered, the constant noise may set off a dialogue in your head about pulling your own child from her perfectly good school and sticking her in that German immersion school down the street that you've passed so many times. Sure, the six-foot-tall teachers who emerge from Das Tagespflege have the warmth of a Sub-Zero fridge, but who doesn't need German fluency in their everyday life? You quickly search your brain to figure out whom you might know connected to Das Tagespflege to help get your child into the class this late in the semester.

Right there: stop. That's acting like a lunatic. And while you've allowed your mind to engage in this lunacy, you've completely forgotten whatever you were actually trying to achieve that day that was productive. And perhaps accidently inhaled a misery Cronut without even chewing.

Not good.

You forgot your original goal, and you've turned into a lunatic in the process. When you're a lunatic, you're not getting any closer to what you really want. And you aren't happy. Lunatics are seldom content.

I tend to turn into a lunatic at precisely 2:00 a.m. My eyes pop open, wide with concern about a series of tasks I haven't achieved. I haven't organized the favors for Greyson's birthday party. I haven't bought the dress pants Thompson needs for his choral concert on Thursday. Or trimmed the baby's eyebrows (can I do that while she's sleeping?).

The way the apartment's air conditioner is humming suddenly doesn't sound right, or smell right. I need to call the HVAC guy immediately (he'll be up, right? Or I can at least leave him a message). I need to check the inspection sticker on the car, which I think expired again, so I will get a ticket for no good reason if I don't remedy that (wait, shoot, I really do think my sticker is expired right now as I write this, dammit). I need to finish this book. Right now, at 2:00 a.m.

And I love to worry about work at this hour. There's always some critical email I could send that would just fix everything! I've been known to rise from bed to write a brilliant email (in the bathroom so that the light from my phone doesn't wake my husband, who, free from lunacy, would try to stop me from hitting send and goad me back into bed).

Here's the best piece of advice you will ever get in your whole life:

Don't send any emails at 2:00 a.m.

I wish I could take my own advice. It's pure gold. PURE GOLD.

There's never been a time, ever once, ever ever ever when I woke up in the morning, looked at my iPhone, checked the sent folder, and said, "Thank God I thought to send that email at 2:00 a.m.! What a great idea that was! In the broad light of day I am delighted with how I worded that stiff rebuke!"

Nope. Instead the next day feels more like this: unable to turn back time, I tiptoe through the day with the painful hangover from my before-dawn tirade, and I try to think of a reason to explain my obvious lunacy.

Like: "My nine-year-old stole my phone in the middle of the night and thought it would be really hilarious to humiliate me by crafting an email that would make my friends or coworkers wonder what medication I take when I'm not at work (or perhaps more accurately what medication I neglected to take). I'm so sorry about that. Please just hit delete."

So to review:

(1) *Don't send emails at 2:00 a.m.*

(2) *Instead, recognize that you probably can't do anything effective about whatever the issue is at 2:00 a.m.* The only other people awake are other lunatics, and morning news anchors who are getting up for their show and wondering how the hell they are going to be perky on that particular day. You might as well table that particular action item for at least a few hours.

(3) *Scribble down your once-in-a-lifetime idea on a pad and let it go until the morning.* If you are certain, as I

usually am, of the sheer genius of the plan you've just hatched while trying to block out your partner's snoring with three pillows, just jot down that bit of wisdom on a piece of paper next to your bed. Chances are that bad boy will keep until morning, when you can judge the pros and cons of shaving your head or selling all your children's possessions from a portable table set up in front of their school to teach them a lesson or going on an all-Triscuit diet (Wait, that last one's not bad! Write that down.).

(4) *Then go back to sleep.* I know that's generally the problem: you can't sleep. But you'd be amazed how much just writing down your problems and questionable solutions will help. Give the problem and solution over to the pad for the night. The person who made up the phrase "Don't make a mountain out of a molehill" coined the saying after her own 2:00 a.m. fret session (that's the truth—I researched it on the Internet and everyone knows that everything you read online is true).

Mind you, not being a lunatic is a work in progress for me. A nonstop journey. A chant I do in the shower in the morning when I'm thinking about lying down on the tile floor and letting the water run over me all day rather than getting out and facing the world.

In fact, my husband just walked by and glanced at the title of the chapter, "Try Not to Be a Lunatic," and dared to say, "How's that going for you?"

He scooted away very quickly when I looked up.

I should also mention that as I write this, I'm sporting a shiner on my right eye that's the result of my first foray into the world of cosmetic fillers. It was not a success. The horrible plight of aging is winning, and handily at that. Sometimes I wish the hands of time would have some mercy and just strangle me rather than torturing me slowly, one horrifying discovery at a time. And adding to the lunacy.

Where was I? Right: don't get distracted.

When your mind is focused, ask yourself the most important question: What's my goal? What am I trying to achieve as a result of all this fretting? What would make me feel better, happier, more fulfilled? Both at 2:00 a.m. and in broad daylight? Losing some weight so I feel better in my clothes? Having something fulfilling to do while the kids are at school? Making more money? Making the other dads jealous of my child's talent?

There's no judgment here. Be really honest with yourself.

What do you actually want?

Strip away the titles. Don't say you'd be happy if you were president of the United States. Why do you want the job? Because you want the ability to unleash nuclear weapons on countries that have gotten on your nerves for decades? Because you want to tell people at your high school reunion that you run the country? Because you want a house with two kitchens? Because if the inspiration is that last one, there are quicker, easier, more efficient ways to achieve that. Calling a builder and doing some remodeling or adding a grill outside with a sink and mini-fridge so it's like a kitchen, while not being easy, is much more straightforward than getting yourself elected as leader of the free world.

If you're honest with yourself about what you are really and truly after, you won't waste a ton of time and energy chasing down a goal that might end up not being satisfying anyway. For example, the White House really has three kitchens. So you would have gone through all the trouble of a primary election, a general election, a swearing-in, moving . . . and then finding out you have one too many kitchens. Total bummer.

Competition can prove a major distraction and obfuscate your real goal. I see this all the time in the news business. Reporters and anchors can be so competitive. They fixate on another talent in the same shop and keep score of what opportunities, assignments, or extra goodies that person is getting that they're not. Then they decide they must have the same thing. I've seen men and women fight for assignments they don't even really want, just to get the gig away from another anchor they feel bent on one-upping. The problem is that once they win the assignment and get out on the road with their microphone and crew to get cracking, they realize they aren't any happier, because that particular beat wasn't their dream. It was someone else's.

My mother used to say: Be careful what you wish for; you just might get it.

Boy is that the truth! That's another way of saying that you better understand what you are really after, what need within yourself you are really trying to fulfill, and address that specifically, before you waste your life chasing a goal that isn't your own. Ask anyone who went to law school to make their parents happy or because they thought going to law school was the thing to do. Those loans are hard to pay off when you finally figure out that being a circus clown is what would really fulfill your dreams. Clowns don't make enough to pay off useless debt. But they have a blast driving those tiny clown cars.

I've brought up the notion of this nagging discontentment with other moms, dads, and even just random people, and so many said, "Why can't we ever just be happy with our achievements? Why are we always striving for more?" Why do we often aspire for more without taking a beat to enjoy or even notice what we already have? I truly believe so much of the problem is not correctly identifying what you really want, what would in truth make you happy. Not the job itself, but what is it about the job that is so appealing? Are you sure that job will deliver on that sensation, if you dedicate your precious hours, days, and years to landing the position? You better be. Why do you want your child in that school? Is the real motive to impress other parents? Because if you shoehorn your kid's way in, and the school isn't actually a good fit for him, he'll be miserable. And other parents aren't impressed when your son is miserable and acting out and failing out, no matter what fantastic, impressive, expensive, impossible-to-get-into-school we are talking about.

Taking the time to really understand and identify the right goal for you is essential to not becoming a lunatic. Then, with the true goal in sight, remember that most of the time life isn't a zero-sum game. Someone else achieving or receiving doesn't mean you won't also. Lots of times there is plenty to go around. Not to belabor the newsroom analogy, but that happens to be where I work (and you may have guessed, the field does in fact boast more than its fair share of lunatics). Lots of news people I've worked with and witnessed take the approach that you have to run down the other talent with your car to get ahead. I will admit I've thought about taking out one or two anchors in the parking lot in my time (especially one in particular—God help me, she's truly not safe crossing the street when I'm at my looniest). But homicide or even just boring old backstabbing really isn't necessary. There are twenty-four hours a day, seven days a week to fill in the world of cable news channels. Lots of airtime to go around. Plus, no matter how good mowing down that one particular coworker might feel in the moment my car makes impact, I'd be in jail pretty quick after that, since I'm not a career criminal and have no cover-up experience. And I'd be much further from whatever I was striving for before that. That's lunatic behavior for sure.

Figure out what you really want, make sure you're honest with yourself about what you're really after and why, so you've got the right goal in your sights, and then focus all your effort on that single goal and don't get distracted. I'm convinced this is the road to happiness and away from total lunacy.

CHAPTER FOUR

SIT DOWN AND TAKE A LOAD OFF

I will never forget the first time I saw one of the hairdressers fasten the fake blonde bun on the back of Karen Grassle's head. The idea that orb of spun gold wasn't naturally hers had never occurred to me. Turns out she had modern locks, bluntly cut, that fell loosely to her shoulders. Those were swept up and hidden, a false donut of hair pinned over the ends.

"What are you looking at, Missy?" she laughed. Karen had a rich, deep voice that could fill a room or a theater. She was trained at the Royal Academy in London. And even as a kid, I could tell. She was so kind to me, always a welcoming smile. But I had the sense she'd seen me many times before. So many Ingalls children had come before me; I imagine the predictability of what I represented, the formula of *Little House*, was wearing a bit thin for her.

By contrast, the Caroline on the screen and the pages of the books never tired, her bright eyes refusing to dim even though she labored around the clock. I just recently reread the *Little House* books and just marveled at Caroline (and then wept and got nauseous). She helps Pa clear the land around the Ingalls homestead with a baby strapped to her chest, and when a log falls on her foot, she presses on with a brave face because she has no choice, really. Later that night, the house finally quiet, she soaks her purple foot in water and then struggles to walk. Don't forget, there was no ibuprofen (or oxycodone) to see her through.

On the show, she was even more irritating and heroically perfect. Ma was up before dawn, collecting the eggs, feeding the animals, tending to the children, and hauling the family into town. Then she'd go to her paying job at Nellie's restaurant, waiting tables and working in the kitchen, before picking up the children at school and walking them back home to get dinner on the table. Then she'd sweep up, wash the dishes, and do some more chores to prep for the next day. And let's not forget they somehow conceived a slew of children in there somewhere. After a typical day like hers, I'd scream, "Get off me! Go sleep on the table!" (They hadn't invented couches yet, or the Ingalls couldn't afford one, I'm not sure which, but there wasn't a stich of comfortable furniture anywhere on that set. Still, that would not have stopped me from sending Charles away so I could get some shut-eye.)

Caroline was the prairie equivalent of today's Supermom or Superwoman: the high-power working gal who somehow never misses drop-off, where she presents her kids with a lunchbox chock full of homemade sushi and hand-pressed carrot juice, after volunteering to be class parent, qualifying for her thirteenth Ironman race, and perfecting the art of applying self-tanner all over her body without creating any streaks or turning her palms orange. She's an utterly impossible ideal, yet way too many of us buy into the notion she's actually the lady standing next to us at back-to-school night.

Too many times, when I'm talking to other moms at school or people who watch me on Fox, they mistake me for one of these super heroes, saying: "You're amazing! Three kids, career in overdrive, hair defrizzed, and a husband. How do you do it all?"

I always respond, "Poorly."

Yes, to the naked eye, I might be the portrait of the woman who has it all. But portraits don't have sound. And our sound is *loud.*

I don't say this to complain, and I certainly wouldn't trade a second of my family-filled chaos for a lifetime of peace, but before another woman does anything like envy my life, she should buy earplugs.

I'm not seamlessly juggling motherhood, a high profile job, and a two-career marriage. I'm just getting by. Just like you, I forget to put the field trip money in my son's backpack and curse myself when I get to work and find the cash folded inside the permission slip stuffed into my purse. I feel like the worst mom who's ever lived, and tell myself for the millionth time, "I'm doing the best I can!" I must say those words a dozen times a day, because that's how many times I feel I've screwed up some critical task and ruined my child's future/hopes for college/digestive tract.

My hat is off to the women (and men) who stay at home taking care of their families full-time. Now that is work. I come to the office on Mondays to get a little peace and quiet after a loud, stressful weekend at home.

That's the dirty little secret of working moms everywhere: *Monday is our Saturday.*

That's the day we leave our squabbling, delightful, yet messy children at home and head to the office to rest and recharge. That's the sweet point of pause on our upside-down calendars. We collapse at our desks on Monday mornings, let out a sigh, and have a cup of coffee.

While it's still hot.

With no one asking for buttered toast with the crusts cut off while they light their sister's hair on fire.

On Mondays, after a second cup of coffee, someone else styles my hair and covers the deep, dark circles under my eyes (thank you, Nicole and JoJo). So when a delightful mother on the field trip works up the courage to ask me how I get my hair to look so perfect all the time, I proudly say, "I don't. Theresa at Fox News does." (While we're speaking of suspiciously perfect hair, you know how supermodel/supermom/superwife/superhuman Giselle Bündchen says she doesn't own a hairbrush? That's not because her super hair doesn't need brushing. It's because SOMEONE ELSE BRUSHES IT!)

You should see what I look like when I show up at work in the morning. I take a shower and throw on some clothes and leave the house with wet hair and no makeup, but the single best perk of my job is that I've got someone like Theresa waiting for me when I get to the office. She waves her magic wand and makes the frizz disappear. She gently tells me when the time has come to give up the deep side part I've had since middle school. Then she cuts, blows, and styles, all while I'm sitting there, motionless, not participating, probably sleeping.

Then our wardrobe maven, Gwen, picks out my clothes and suggests a nice pair of Spanx to make sure the monochromatic, suction-cup-like dress laid out for me doesn't bulge. And sometimes she'll quietly suggest two pairs of Spanx if we happen to be around the holiday season. Or summer barbeque season. Or spring or fall.

I'm pretty sure the people at school think there are two blonde women who hover around my kids. There's the woman at drop-off who's disheveled, blotchy, and running after her children with the musical instrument that was abandoned in the backseat of the car, and then there's the woman at pickup who looks as if she spent the day having each eyelash individually painted by a glam squad.

One morning, we were running horribly late, probably because I left the house without my phone (or my keys or one of my children). We had to march, heads hung, to the principal's office for another dreaded Late Note. We stood in The Line of Shame that forms in front of Mrs. Rodriguez's desk with the other families, muttering about evil trash trucks and forgotten lunches.

When our turn came, I said, "I'm so sorry we're late. I guess I need a late slip for the boys."

Mrs. Rodriguez looked at me as if I were vaguely familiar, perhaps someone she'd known in high school or seen at the grocery store.

"You are their . . . aunt?" she asked.

I said, "Mrs. Rodriguez, it's me."

Her eyes went wide with horror, and I feel awful that I'm doubling down on her embarrassment by sharing the story. But the tale is the best way to illustrate the dramatic contrast in my daily, physical transformation. I've seen many TV people publish terrifying photos of themselves without makeup. Mrs. Rodriguez will tell you that, for me, that move would be career ending.

Before you compare yourself to me or any other perky person on television, in magazines, or at pickup, remember, you didn't see that woman when she woke up and you have no idea what's happened and who has helped since then.

So before you measure yourself as less than, please know that you are most likely all that and more.

I confess all this to help debunk the Myth of the Superwoman, a fantasy that has way too many of us lying awake at night, browbeating ourselves as if we were the target of an FBI investigation. There's a real danger in holding ourselves to an impossible standard. Whether it's Caroline Ingalls or Kelly Ripa. How could any viewer not feel less than by comparison?

When we constantly thirst for what we don't have and vow to achieve what we haven't conquered, we fail to enjoy what's right in front of us: the joy of our children, the love of our families, the pleasures of today (eating chocolate). We make ourselves—and everyone who lives with us—miserable, neurotic messes.

That's why, when I listen to any of today's Superwomen telling ladies everywhere we can have it all if we just try a little harder, if we just "lean in," I let out a long, deep sigh. I want to hand the other women who are listening—and now covered in nervous hives—a nice glass of boxed wine and say, "Here's my advice: Don't lean in. In fact, sit down and take a load off."

I want to sing and chant that hive-relieving mantra from the rooftops, and take out a full-page ad in every paper. I'm going to have my new catchphrase printed on T-shirts. My sons tell me everyone has to have a catchphrase now. It's the thing. I'm calling dibs on this one. I will stamp it on coffee mugs and drink cozies. I'm not even kidding. And I'm going to sell all this merch online, with T-shirts in every shape and size. (Go look right now. I'm selling all this stuff. The proceeds will go to buy fed-up women cases of Mommy's Time Out Pinot Grigio, which is awesome, by the way.)

My mother always told me I could be anything I wanted. "You could keep acting, or you could be the first woman president of the United States," she'd say. "Or a doctor! Or an astronaut! Anything you want." So as a girl, I pictured myself in the White House with my husband and children, with a stethoscope around my neck, so I could continue to see patients when I wasn't too busy running the country and winning wars. And then I'd juggle my schedule here and there, so I could pop out of Washington and guest star on an episode of *Knots Landing*.

Some dreams die hard. And some merely evaporate when they bump up against reality. Even if they would have let me take the nuclear launch codes with me to the set of *Knots Landing*, I hadn't budgeted any time to ever do school pickup. I had zero idea about what we now annoyingly like to call work-life balance.

My best friend from childhood, Cori, used to talk about one day becoming a child psychologist and starting a private practice that would allow her to work more or less, depending on how much time she wanted and needed to spend with her kids. She said something completely ridiculous about her career being portable (like being president isn't portable? You can whip that out anywhere)! I always thought she was selling herself short. She was limiting herself and her true potential. Why not reach for the stars? Astronauts have families too!

Well, guess what. Cori is one of my few female friends from childhood or college who remains in the professional workforce. She knew something the rest of us had just glossed over. Gloria Steinem told us: career, career, career. We had all the time in the world to have kids and find a partner. Start climbing that ladder, chica!

But I wish I had considered, right at that very moment, that I might want a career or a job path that could be dialed up and dialed back, depending on my priorities at the time. When our kids are small, they need our attention almost all of the time. Work might take a backseat. There are careers that allow workers to adjust their hours to fit their lives. Some professions where you provide client services, like accounting, bookkeeping, legal services, writing contracts, writing or editing, can be controlled simply by increasing or limiting the number of clients or assignments you take on at one time. Yes, you pay a price as a lawyer if you aren't on the partner track, and that price is that you probably won't become a partner. But the flip side is that if you take time off or scale back hours when you have kids, you do in fact have a valuable vocation when you need or want to go back to work. It will take a lot of work to build back clients and business, but at least you have a plan of action you can visualize.

Beyond just your profession, more and more modern employers respect that both moms and dads hunger for this flexibility. Amazon is experimenting with a thirty-hour work week. The openings pay less, but they provide full benefits. Banks on Wall Street allow job sharing, where workers split the week with other like-minded people who want to work part-time, at least for the moment. This is just a sample of the paths I might have considered, knowing that when my kids got bigger and spent breakfast to nearly dinner at school and playing sports, I could press down on the pedal at work and increase my hours and commitment. There are pluses and minus to all of this, of course. You may miss out on being the top gun in your field, having passed up hours, clients, assignments, and income. But you had the joy of your children, and they had you. Life is made up of trade-offs.

But I didn't think about those tough choices, the inevitable forks in the road, what was truly possible given that we can only be in one place at one time, and most of my friends didn't either. And now I notice that many formerly hard-charging women have raised the white flag and retired to the sidelines. I mentioned this to Television Goddess Megyn Kelly recently over dinner. If you own a television or live on this planet, you certainly know she's the breakout Fox News talent that everyone on Earth is talking about. What you may not know is that while Megyn is a force of nature on her side of the anchor desk, cutting to the heart of every argument and skewering any guest who tries to feed her audience a pack of lies, she's also a dirt-under-the-fingernails, hands-on mom. She's the mom who starts the meal on her feet cutting all her kids' food into bite-size cubes and finishes with two kids on her lap and one dangling from her neck. All while she effortlessly carries the adult conversation.

But she's also human. And Wray and I love hanging out with Megyn and her husband, Doug, because we love to compare our collective body of slipups and disasters as parents. You can't be a parent without the ability to laugh at yourself, or you'll jump off a bridge. (Plus we love the same television programs they do, so there's a whole night of conversation right there.)

So I mentioned this notion to Megyn, telling her about two women I know, the wives of two of New York's biggest power brokers. Both of these women had high-octane careers to kill for and impressive degrees before they married their husbands and started their families. Both decided to stay home full-time to raise their children, due in large part to the fact that their husbands' careers were so demanding, someone had to be available when the school nurse called to let them know some nice friend had poured glue in their child's ear. And while all of their offspring are model human beings, moving about the planet in ways that would surely make a mother burst with pride, each woman has confided in me that her biggest regret in life had to do with ditching her job and not keeping

at least a toehold in the career she'd worked so hard
to get up and running. Decades later, neither woman
could see a way back in, and as their children became
increasingly allergic to their presence the way that all
kids do, they lamented this decision more and more.

"Why is it," Megyn wondered, "that for so many
women *it's full-throttle or nothing*?"

As usual, she instantly articulates the essential
question. Another reason why in my fondest dreams
I'm Gayle to her Oprah.

To me, this all-or-nothing mentality is another un-
intended consequence of the Lean In Culture. Many
internalize the message to mean that if you aren't the
CEO, if you aren't demanding at least as much cash as
your male counterpart (if not more), you're a failure.
So why lean at all? Forget it. Nordstrom is having a
fantastic sale anyway.

I know what you're thinking. "She's a fine one to
talk!" This is what we say to the woman talking. We
attack her for giving advice or just bitching out loud,
because the woman talking (or writing) has the time
to use a pen and paper without a child dumping yogurt on her head or a boss telling her she didn't wipe
down her station properly. (For the record, I am, in
fact, wearing banana yogurt in my hair while I'm typing this.)

I hear you, sister! In the spirit of that sentiment,
let me give you my disclaimers. You've already heard

most of them, mostly that my job provides a ton of perks that give me the appearance of juggling a thousand balls at once, when in reality that neat trick is made possible by an enormous mostly invisible team and a crazy ton of Photoshop. And my husband carries a massive amount of the weight. Quite literally, in fact: as far as the kids are concerned, my arms are for ornamental purposes only. He does all the carrying and assembling. And quite a lot of volunteering at school.

I only mean to turn on the hazard lights for women who hop off the work treadmill only to jump on the one marked "family track" and crank up the speed. Ten or fifteen years down the road, when your children's lives are filled with teenage things, Mom is a Drag. I've noticed that women who went from full-throttle careers to full-throttle motherhood find themselves at loose ends, unclear where to direct the wellspring of energy, their career paths having stretched on down the road without them.

When did slowing down the pace become as shameful as binge eating? Is the choice really between CEO or stay-at-home parent? Why has the Mommy Track gotten such a bad rap? Maybe we could just hire a crisis PR team to give the Mommy Track a new name, and we'd all feel better about it. "Exclusive" and "Celebrity" are two words our society falls to its collective knees over. I'm just workshopping ideas here, but I'm thinking something along the lines of: The Secret,

Star-Studded, Organic, Gluten-Free, Red-Carpet Hik-
ing Trail to Harmonious Yoga-Like Bliss That Nine
Out of Ten Beverly Hills Doctors Recommend. Too
long? Just right?

Now I know there are moms, both single and married, shaking a frustrated fist at a conversation about
choosing whether to work outside the home. They are
working to feed their families, not to be on the cover
of *Forbes*. They don't have the luxury of pondering the
pluses and minuses of punching a timecard. Let me be
perfectly clear, so there can be no misunderstanding:
all those moms, and dads for that matter, are heroic
and deserving of the utmost respect.

Come on! As a species, we are so hard on each
other. I hate that when I'm standing in a group of
moms, and I want to ask the woman next to me about
herself, because I'm trying to be friendly and just
strike up a normal conversation, but the phrasing of
the question is like walking through a minefield with
snipers' rifles trained on the secret meaning behind
every word. I cannot ask, as a man would, "So . . .
what do you do for a living?" If she doesn't work outside the home, but instead labors all day for the health
and happiness of her family, her response is either an
apologetic, "I'm a stay-at-home mom," or she wants to
smack me in the face because she mistakenly thinks
I'm judging her with my question.

Almost inevitably, we all walk away feeling
judged. Which is why I instead ask where she got

her cute purse. Now that's a deep and meaningful conversation.

The painful truth is that I am too selfish to stay at home full-time. I can admit that even though I feel very guilty about that fact, which obviously makes me a bad person. To that point, I usually warn moms who are going back to work after having their first baby that being a working parent means feeling guilty all the time.

All the time. I'm dead serious.

I feel guilty when I'm not with my kids, and someone else is taking abuse about the desirability of the snack they've prepared or bathing in the sunshine of their sweet smiles (you've pretty much got a fifty-fifty shot of abuse or smiles on a good day).

And I also feel guilty when I'm the one in the trenches. I feel the weight of the work I've left unfinished at the office. The never-ending internal conflict is the ultimate Catch-22. I'm damned no matter what, cursing myself no matter what, feeling that I've let someone down no matter what!

I feel guilty ALL THE TIME.

I know I'm not alone. I've brought women to tears just uttering that lone sentence (right above) that rings so true to far too many.

I've started calling this the Working Mom's Perma-Guilt, but another mom recently corrected me. "Oh, it's not just working moms," Karina assured me.

We were sitting at another chorus recital at school, waiting (150 years) for the kids to take the stage. I was using the free second not to breathe but to check the work emails that were multiplying like rabbits on my iPhone (and I was feeling guilty about having left work early, obviously).

"I feel guilty all the time that I stopped working. What was all that college and training for? All that time and money and work? And then nòt using it!" She threw her hands up in the air. I was about to shout "Amen, sister!" and order another round of drinks, but then I remembered we were in a church pew at our kids' Catholic school. Shoot.

"That's some guilt," she added.

And she works part-time! And raises her kids! Yet she found time to contribute a new category of Mom Guilt I hadn't considered: Could-Be-Working-More-Hours-Mom-Guilt. (I gotta work on a better name for that one.)

Another mom chimed in, "What about the guilt from depending on your husband for money? All that pressure on him to pay the bills. I feel guilty about that."

Ladies, my Lord. We have got to give ourselves a break. Please.

In fairness, I know my husband feels the Working Mom Guilt, or Parent Guilt. He hates missing a single moment of our kids' lives. Hates it! And I've never seen a more diligent and devoted worker at the office. So he feels guilty wherever he is too.

The only answer I've found, a decade into my glorious and highly emotional tour of duty as a mom, is to try to be completely present in the moment I'm in, wherever that is, and to relish that second in time as precious and fleeting.

⊷⊶ ⊚⊷⊶

I began to write this book after the birth of my daughter. I didn't feel the weight of my own gender as the mother of sons. But with Gemma, I know she will judge my choices and either embrace them or reject them as the road she will never travel. She's watching closely, and not just when I'm preparing her snack. Though she's all over that too.

As I've written and mentioned, my own mother and I had a very complicated relationship to say the least. But I would never be stupid enough to throw everything she said and did in the trash heap. For example, here's one of her best bits of wisdom: "Never lose your ability to support your family," she used to say. "You may be blessed with a partner who does well. Good for you. But he could drop dead tomorrow. You have no idea what the future holds. You have to be able to feed, clothe, and educate your children alone at the drop of a hat. Not replace your partner's income dollar for dollar. That's not necessarily realistic. But if you have to mop floors to put your kids through college, that's your obligation. Be ready for it."

That just makes good sense. As my close friend Jill says very succinctly, because she's a TV producer and knows we are inevitably up against a hard break: "You need a backup to the backup, and then another backup." She is a damn fine producer because she always has as many plans ready as I have pairs of Spanx (also very key).

Being instantly employable doesn't mean you are currently working. But you know what you'd do tomorrow if you're partner came home tonight and said, "So I finally slugged my manager, who is such a complete idiot. God, that felt good! What's for dinner?"

Or if he didn't come home at all.

If I got laid off, I'd be more than willing to bag groceries tomorrow to put food on the table. I've worked a lot of jobs in my lifetime, and I'm hardly afraid to get my hands dirty. Obviously, in terms of dollars per hour, we'd all prefer to have a trade. A bookkeeper can always find work, I'd imagine, and get paid more per hour. Those math dorks know what they are doing. But regardless of the digits on the check, knowing that you can get paid, and tomorrow, is empowering, and I will drill that into the heads of all my children, regardless of gender.

Many years after my mother planted the seed that I needed to be able to hop on a payroll in an instant, I heard the same idea from one of my closest friends from college, Michelle. Apparently her mother was peddling the same wisdom.

Today, Michelle is one of those loving mothers who teases her kids to keep them from thinking they've got the world by the tail too early, but the moment they are out of earshot, marvels at their obvious genius. Back when we met, she was just starting down the road to become a doctor. She had a special knack with kids that told me she'd strike gold as a pediatrician—not a bad skill set to have in your back pocket as a parent, either. (Some lucky guy would really be getting the whole package.)

But as we grew older, I began to see the brilliance of Michelle's career choice, especially compared to other women coming out of schools like Harvard, who had shouted, "It's the C-suite or bust!" and immediately began climbing the corporate ladder like a mudder hell, bent on getting to the top of a wet, sloppy racecourse, with no thought of how a few kids would slow down their course time.

Michelle had smoked out a career that used her brain and skills but didn't eclipse her shot at being a mom—much like my friend Cori. Consciously or not, Michelle chose a job that would allow her to raise a family on her own terms. She can take care of her kids, and everyone else's too. That's pretty damn clever.

But this is not a conversation we had in college. At least most of my friends didn't. Perhaps I was a freak surrounded by other freaks, but we were just dreaming of breaking every glass ceiling we could. Cori is the only one I remember articulating the idea that one day we may have to find a way to punch a time card and pack a lunch in the same morning.

I hate the phrase "work-life balance." It makes me think of hot, sticky Bikram yoga. But I will find a way to articulate the idea to all my kids somewhere between the playground and college when they are deciding what they want to be when they grow up.

I guess my speech will go something like this: The first step, and maybe the most daunting, is to figure out what life will make you sincerely happy. Or even better, make you feel content (peaceful contentment is wildly underrated in our thrill-seeking society). That might be family and career, just career and no family, a partner with no kids, or life as a starving artist on a deserted island inhabited only by turtles. Whatever! I will tell them to do their best to identify and define that image, without giving two bits about what society, friends, or even parents (gulp) think.

Then I will ask them to have some thoughts about a backup plan (hat tip to Jill). To know what they would do to make money in a jam. Beyond that, I would urge them to relish the bits of bliss in every day, the crisp mornings spent on the swings, the natural chatter that fills the car on the way to school, or the carefree weeknight dinners that are spent with your spouse before you have kids to divide your attention. They are always there, though they can be easily eclipsed by clouds if you let them. Happy moments are precious but abundant if you stop to look for them. Don't waste a single one.

Life is like that crazy organ grinder guy with the monkey on his shoulder that no one has ever seen in real life. Your career is the weird accordion he's playing, expanding and contracting to make a few coins, create some happy music, and still leave time to feed and bathe the monkey (okay . . . this analogy went off the rails). Even if you put the accordion on the shelf for a while, you need to be able to dust the thing off in a hurry.

I hope my kids can see that I've tried to put my money where my mouth is. I've been blessed with a cool job that I love, and make no mistake, I work very hard. But I still am certain to slip out to their school to take my turn as Mystery Reader and never miss a school performance no matter the time of day, and that in these moments nothing ever feels more electric than the enormous smile on my child's face when I walk into the classroom and that little person leaps into my arms, thrilled that I've come to surprise them.

I'm not pretending to be Superwoman. I'm not even a fan. And to be honest, I'm not sure Superwoman has very many friends. Everyone I know hates her. She's really quite annoying. She reminds us mere mortals of our fat thighs and inability to lift heavy objects above our waists. Whenever you see that person with the perfect family, the perfect job, the perfect elbows . . . don't you just want to run her down with your car?

God bless you if you are truly the woman who effortlessly has it all. But I have a theory that a lot of women who answer the casting call for Feminist Icon are full of crap in at least a few areas of their life. They do the humble brag. They say, "I didn't get this way overnight!" Or, "I was born ugly! With glasses on! You should see my high school yearbook!"

Notice she just worked her way around to how fit and fabulous she is now. Super Annoying. I guess she also doesn't know that motherhood isn't a competition. Anytime anyone ventures to comment on the struggles or blessings of being a mom, there are a couple dozen bloggers and tweeters with their fingers at the ready to tear that poor mom to shreds, criticize her every move, word, or decision. Why are we doing battle with each other? Who started the Mommy Wars? And how soon can some neutral party like Ellen DeGeneres or Winnie the Pooh negotiate a cease-fire? The very least we could do is commiserate, if not celebrate and support, each other.

To Superwomen and wannabes everywhere, lose the cape. And if someone offers one to you, use the damn thing to clean up the next spill. Because when we constantly vow to look fabulous leaping tall buildings in a single bound, we stumble past the joy that's right in front of us, on level ground: the love, pleasure, and joy of the messy, imperfect life we already have.

CHAPTER FIVE

MICHAEL LANDON: THE ORIGINAL (CHEAPEST) HOLLYWOOD ENTREPRENEUR

I've spent my career in journalism covering some of the boldest, cleverest, and most innovative CEOs in the world, only to come to realize I'd worked for one of the best, way back in Hollywood. Michael Landon cut his teeth on television in *Bonanza*. But he quickly realized to make a mint, he had to be the boss. To own the show. To sell the distribution. To control the purse strings. And in order to keep the money that *Little House* generated, Michael did the lion's share of the heavy lifting on and around the set. He wrote, directed, produced, and starred in the show, at a time when almost no one was doing that and "executive producer" was a job, not a title that served as a perk to ten people on the same production.

From there, he stole just about everything that worked from *Bonanza*. A bunch of dudes with guns being real men on horses, surrounded by pretty women who flashed huge smiles of admiration, and very clear themes and morals about right and wrong, good and bad. Bad never won out, as I've mentioned (sometimes they would fake it so the fight looked close, though, just for good measure). Also, if you needed to fill a few minutes, you could blast the music and everyone could stare longingly into the sunset or at a beautiful outdoor scene. Bubbling brooks were ideal tension breakers when lit properly. The formula might have been predictable, but predictable feels damn good when you're sitting in front of the TV at the end of a long, hard workday. Just look ask the fans of *CSI* and *Law & Order* and *NCIS*.

He did throw in some additional not-so-subtle sex appeal to hook the female audience. Am I the only one who thought his prairie pants were a little tight? Or that his shirt was always (for no reason) mostly unbuttoned, revealing a few too many tufts of chest hair? I certainly didn't notice him as a child, but I saw the ladies on the set simper when he strutted his stuff across the studio.

And in perhaps his shrewdest move as a television impresario, he based the new show on a popular series of books with a built-in, multigenerational audience before the cameras even started rolling. Seriously, what little girl who loved the books was not going to watch?

Add to all that the fact that he was cheap as hell, tight with a buck like I'd never known—always, always, always with an eye on the bottom line. We'd rehearse until we had the scene down so we wouldn't waste a frame of expensive film. "Cut and print!" was the phrase that stretched a big grin across his lips, especially when he got to say that after the first take, signaling that he'd wasted no film getting that scene in the bank.

I've mentioned that he treated the crew with respect and charmed them with his boisterous laugh and dirty jokes meant only for their ears. But then, in a blink of an eye, he'd put on his serious director's face, look through the lens, and get down to business. Everyone on the set worshipped him, so they would throw themselves into their work too, copying him. He drove a well-oiled machine, and 99 percent of us were grateful to be on board and working every muscle we had to keep the money machine rolling. So when he needed one more take before he lost the sunlight, but after the crew should have kicked into overtime pay, the union boss would look the other way, and we'd squeeze in the final scene, fast and to perfection. Saving Michael money. A favor to a friend. He'd pay the union guys back with decades of steady employment in a business where job security was completely unheard of.

Sure there were bad apples in the bunch; there always are. But they cropped up rarely, and when they did, they risked the collective ire of the rest the group, whose glares read, "Don't ruin this for the rest of us!" And the person either got shamed back into line or got fired.

And the peloton cycled on in happy and efficient unison.

On many other sets, you might see big lines of bloated Winnebago dressing rooms, one per star, with each star lounging in his or her own spacious rig. Many big-name players had such accommodations built into their contracts. Not on *Little House*. Michael hired utilitarian Honeywagons, with four small dressing rooms per truck. The rooms were temperature-controlled and had their own bathrooms, but they were so small you'd be lucky to fit one extra person in the dressing room with you.

"Michael Landon" would be written in black erasable marker on the very first dressing room. He was the biggest star, but his dressing room was the same size as mine, the same size as a featured guest performer. The message here was unmistakable. If an eight-by-twelve-foot room is good enough for Michael, that damn room is plenty good enough for you. He lived and worked by example. And saved himself money to boot.

Not that he was allergic to luxury. He drove a racing green Lamborghini from his Malibu mansion to the lot in Culver City every day. He spent money where he liked and saved everywhere else he could. He was generous at the holidays but watched every nickel on regular days, from costumes to craft services to masking tape. I loved that he called me One-Take Missy, but underneath his praise for my ability to get a scene right on the first take was his appreciation for keeping down the costs of production. He was always looking at ways we could group two outdoor scenes, to capture the same light, and encouraging the costume and makeup people to be at the ever-ready so we could do a quick change before starting in on a new scene.

There was an economy to everything. And to me that steady discipline from the adult in charge was new.

⊸═◉ ◉═⊷

When I was five or six, I received a royal blue lockbox as a gift. There was a slot on top where I could stuff my coins and carefully folded bills without having to open the combination lock on the front. Once, a director gave me a five-dollar bill, folded like a beautiful origami swan, for a scene I'd done particularly well. I had to unlock the box to get that prize inside. There was no way to jam the bird through the coin slot. But I never spent that sucker, and most of the money didn't see the light of day again. I hated to spend even a dollar, except in a real bind, so I kept the loot safely tucked away—only counting the total alone, behind a locked bathroom door.

That box was my tiny piece of financial security. My nest egg. Very occasionally, I'd crack open the safe to pay the guy from Numero Uno Pizza when we'd ordered a pie and my mother realized (too late) that she didn't have enough cash in her purse to pay.

Other than that, I was a hoarder (before that had odd cachet).

My family was not loaded, but we were not poor either, not by a long shot. I grew up in a suburb of Los Angeles called Porter Ranch, deep in the valley that Moon Unit Zappa made famous. Yes, my sister, Tiffany, and I were original Valley Girls.

Like, totally.

My family lived in a tract home in a suburb that was the real-life set for the movie *E.T.* The flying bicycle chase scene with *E.T.* in the basket covered by a blanket was shot right down the street from where I grew up. I don't know if you remember the houses speeding by, but what you saw was miles and miles of homes where there was an identical pattern of the same four houses repeating over and over and over. That's what tract homes are. The same four or five over and over and over. My friends and I used to watch the film and shout every time the wheels sped past a home that was the same model as one of ours. They shot *Poltergeist* not too far away too. I guess Steven Spielberg thought our neighborhood was both generic and creepy.

We moved into our white stucco home before the front lawn had a chance to grow in, and we were surrounded by other young families who wanted to live on a cul-de-sac where kids could play without getting mowed down by traffic.

The schools were good, the crime was nonexistent, and there was a gas station, an Alpha Beta supermarket, and a Jack in the Box drive-through at the bottom of our hill, so we had everything covered. This should have been a cozy nest of security.

But my parents had an unusual way of organizing our finances. They didn't.

My dad used to say that Los Angeles is a one-industry town, and that industry isn't building cars or clearing out coal mines, it's Show Business. He loves that phrase, I think because the name sounds a little silly and when you say it, you can practically hear people singing, "There's no business like show business like no business I know!"

What he meant was that if you paint, you paint background scenery. If you drive a truck, you drive a prop truck between shooting locations. If you practice law, you better be damn good at talent contracts.

When he originally came to California from Chicago after college, he worked as an aeronautical engineer who turned rocket parts into space shuttle parts at Jet Propulsion Laboratory (very 1960s *Mad Men*). But Hollywood eventually sucked him in too, and he found his way from Lockheed Martin to sound engineering, designing theaters and sound systems for studios and movie houses, at the helm of his own small company.

Our family was kind of a bizarre mash up of the 1950s gender roles. My dad worked all day and came home on Friday and handed his paycheck to my mother. That was the end of his job on the family financial front. He'd turn around and go back to work on Monday.

He loved to tell people to go to hell—one reason he was his own boss, my mother told me more than a million times. He didn't like to be told what to do. He'd cop to that for sure. But that does limit the number of people you can work for if you aren't willing to follow orders.

Meanwhile, my mother was, to say the least, an extremely controlling person, and controlling the purse strings was the ultimate power. She alone decided how much to spend, on what, and when. She loved to say yes, and she adored saying no, or even better, giving you her terms to get to yes.

Lots of power there.

The problem was that she ran our household like a banana republic. She spent wildly when we were flush, never socking away funds for the times when the banana crop failed. Our boom and bust cycles were epic.

Early on in their marriage, my mother decided to make my sister and me the family's backup source of income. Of course, that was not the main reason she started dragging us to auditions for movies and modeling. She was also dazzled by the attention, aspiration, and admiration. What a great way to stick it to the family she'd left behind in New Jersey—tell them to turn on the television at noon, or open to page sixteen in a magazine, and see her beautiful daughters on display. That certainly proved who won!

But the money from our acting and modeling jobs gave my mother a great deal of pleasure as well. Certainly she had no right to wildly spend our earnings however she liked. That money was supposed to sit in a trust fund until we were eighteen—to be used for college, she would say. Except it almost never works that way in real life, at least not in my day, not in our house. Instead my mother seemed to feel free to write checks from the checking account bearing my name. When no one batted an eye, she took that as permission to continue.

To be sure, all the money she spent went to shower my sister and me with bits of heaven. Private schools, birthday parties, dance lessons, horseback riding, Guess jeans (when they were very cool and skin-tight with zippers on the outside of the ankles and Anna Nicole Smith was still named Vickie Lynn).

The money bought all the extras that we loved but didn't need. And that's perhaps one of the reasons she didn't see herself as doing anything wrong.

She also believed, with reason, that the paychecks were as much hers as ours. She had a point. She was the one who took us for head shots, hired and fired our agents, managed the schedules, drove us to auditions, put the right outfits in the backseat of the car for us to change into after school, listened to us carp and complain about how we were too tired to go on another audition, lectured us about how lucky we were to even get the call, styled our hair, taught us our lines, sat outside while we went in and read for producers, drove us home afterward, and did the whole entire thing again from scratch if we got a callback. Whew.

If we booked a job, she was required by law to be there on set, managing us every single minute. And still, in the eyes of the law, she did all that for free.

That's not fair. Just ask Kris Jenner.

Trouble was, my mother spent money like water. With no plan for the next week. If we booked a job, we went shopping. When I got hired as a series regular, ponies rained from the sky. But when a dry spell hit? Watch out. We'd abandon clothes at the dry cleaner rather than pay the bill.

During the leaner times, I felt pressure to book work. But Hollywood doesn't operate like that. When you're hot, there aren't enough days in the week to fit the bookings and offers. Work breeds more work. Everyone wants you. Or no one does. Lukewarm cools to ice cold in a heartbeat.

And that does not feel good.

Imagine for a moment that this is the life of an eight-year-old, who wins the part of her young lifetime when she joins the fictional Ingalls family, one of television's most popular, longest-running shows. Without question, this job was an economic boon, a banana bumper crop. A game changer—for a time, at least. Make no mistake, the paycheck was second, icing on the cake really. The true prize was temporary, superstardom. My father always said that in our whole lives

One of my first few days on *Little House*, shooting on location in Sonora, California, where the Coopers' wagon took its epic tumble.

Ma and Pa Cooper with me, getting ready to shoot a scene just before the fatal wagon accident that would make my character an orphan.

Charles and Albert prepare to park their wagon dramatically across the tracks to stop the steaming locomotive that was taking Cassandra and James to an orphanage.

Filming a morning scene in Simi Valley, California, still in my costume nightgown, without those signature braids (whoa, that's a lot of hair!).

Rachel Greenbush, one of the twins who played Carrie Ingalls, with me playing in a dressing room between scenes.

Jason Bateman, who played my brother James, with me in front of a prop truck on the Simi Valley set. I'm sure I was hoping our next scene would incude hand holding.

My grand-mother, who took almost all the photos I have from the set, with Melissa Gilbert. She especially loved this picture because she adored Melissa.

The only person Grandma liked better than Melissa Gilbert: Michael Landon.

Me in front of one of the enormous trucks that carried all the modern gear to make our set look authentic. I loved that the tires were nearly as tall as I was.

Michael in front of our delicious food truck, showing us why the ladies always loved him.

Karen Grassel, who played Caroline Ingalls or Ma, holding the sunglasses she wouldn't be able to wear in the scene, since they weren't invented in prairie days.

Katherine MacGregor, who played Harriet Oleson and had as much pizzazz off camera as on. Always larger than life.

Lining up for graduation in Harvard Yard with my friend Michelle.

Filling in on a weekend edition of *The Five* at Fox
when some of the regular cast needed a break.

Everyone who made our miracle possible: Briana's family and mine, with baby Gemma in the center, just where she belongs.

Our first holiday card photo with Gemma. They are all laughing at me because I'm telling them to smile for the camera and be quiet, which never happened.

together, he'd never seen my mother happier than when I was working on *Little House*. She squired me around the San Fernando Valley like a treasured doll to be admired by jealous friends and curious strangers alike. And she spent cash as if I'd never be out of work again.

Not a great choice on her part. Because the nature of acting is that unemployment lurks at the end of every season, the day after every wrap party. Actors are always just about to be fired or cancelled, even on the first day. Being out of work was as inevitable as time marching forward. I could see the unemployment line just around the corner. I had no idea why she could never see what I saw, but her lack of vision on this front made me nervous. All the time. At a time in my life when most kids don't even understand the concept of money.

A decade later, long after *Little House*, as well as way too many more boom-and-bust cycles, I began to apply to colleges. I had a clear picture of what I wanted: security. But that didn't mean boredom. Hollywood had ruined me for regular life. I was looking for something with a little pizzazz. But even more than that, I wanted a steady paycheck with my name printed right on the front. There's tremendous power in having someone hand you money for a job well done. A rush. A sense of independence, knowing you can create your own security without anyone else, a way to ease your own worry.

All this led me to news. A job in front of the camera, where I controlled the content, used my brain, wrote the words I would say, could be inquisitive and creative, but perhaps have a long, steady career where I didn't need to pray for my show to be renewed each year, if I was ever even lucky enough to get another series. This career path seemed to check all the boxes. And of course that desirability and demand meant loads of people wanted to break in.

To get started in news, you sort of have to know someone, someone who can help you get a foot in the door, get your résumé pulled from the massive pile that comes flooding into the decision maker even when there's no opening and no decision to be made. Sadly, I didn't know a soul. Not a field producer, not a security guard, not a janitor. So I realized in order to network and meet people whom I could convince I was a good risk, I needed to work as an intern. Work for free. Nooooo! But alas I had no choice. That started with doing the internship with Carol Breshears at Fox in LA. But that was only the beginning. I was going to need to meet many more people before I could actually land that first (golden yet minimum wage) job. This is one of the reasons that you hear so many beauty queens say they want to "read the news on TV" after pageant life and then you never see or hear from them again. The drudgery of breaking into the business and landing a paying job is tough as hell.

As if that weren't enough, I had another huge obstacle to test just how badly I wanted this career. The year after I worked for Carol, I landed another unpaid job working for the NBC News bureau in Washington, DC. Sure, this was a plumb gig: I could prove desire and maybe smarts to a slew of people who knew and influenced news directors in affiliates around the country in small markets where someone might actually pay me (very little) money. But the idea did not exactly sit well with my mother. The last thing on the planet she wanted was for me to make a life away from acting and away from her. So she told me she wouldn't give me a dime of support for a summer of free work.

I'm not trying to peddle a sob story here or make the case that I should have been allowed to work for peanuts. Actually, peanuts would have been an improvement—at least I could have eaten them. Lots of kids have to get paying jobs to work their way through college and pay the entire tuition bill themselves, every single dime. But I was trying to switch my star and shine in a different galaxy. And that summer looked like a perfect opportunity for my mom to hook her lasso on one of those points and wrestle back control of the whole operation.

Fat chance.

What I needed big time was to make money in short order, and the only place hiring at that moment was the dorm's underground kitchen. That sounded fine until I got down there and bathed in the steam that was poaching everyone with a cooking utensil in their hand. I may have put on a hairnet, but I didn't need one because every strand on my body was glued to my skin and not going anywhere.

The facilities department paid minimum wage for me to chop vegetables underneath the rooms where my fancy classmates slept. Picture mountains of carrots and piles of potatoes diced into petite blocks. And the mountains needed to reach the ceiling to feed everyone. I didn't notice any Kardashians or Hiltons working down there. But I needed money. What could I do? I was lucky to find anything this late in the school year. The only other openings were on the dorm crew, cleaning other students' toilets and sinks. The kids who worked those jobs were the true heroes. I decided to stick with this sticky job over that one.

I was a few weeks into the job when one of my classmates saw me coming up from the kitchen in my black-and-white checked kitchen uniform and, as if in slow motion, recognized what the hideous outfit meant. She then recoiled in horror, but not before asking me what I was doing in those clothes.

"Actually, I was making your lunch," I responded defiantly.

"SHUT UP!" she said, taking the words right out of my mouth.

"Yep. I need to make some cash in a hurry, so I can do an unpaid internship in DC this summer. My mom isn't too thrilled that I'm not coming home, so I've got to hustle up the dough myself, no pun intended," I said, laughing lightly.

"Wow, my mother would never do that! But I have to hand it to you. No internship would ever be worth that to me," she sniffed, turning on her heel, and strutting away.

No, in fact I knew no internship was worth that to her. Okay, yes, I was humiliated. I was ashamed that I needed money that badly and that she was spitting on my shoes for going to the basement to earn it. But I wasn't standing on the street corner turning tricks for Christ's sake! And a big chunk of me was proud that I was willing to wield a knife and endure her scorn for what mattered to me—and that she was too fancy or too lazy to do the same. Less competition for me.

I also knew in my heart she was wrong. The polyester pants didn't prove I was worth less; in fact, they proved just the opposite. I'd gotten my first taste of a paycheck before I could read the writing on its face, and ever since I'd always gotten a thrill of pride when someone outside the family was willing to part with their cash in exchange for honest work I could provide. Like, "Me? You think what I'm doing here is worth money? Okay!"

When I left for Washington, DC, that summer, I showed my mother who had the power. (Snap! I've Got the Power!) And, wise to the notion she'd lost the battle but not yet the war, she added to the money

I'd saved in the kitchen (and everywhere else I could make a buck that spring) and made my adventure a lot easier.

Before I left, though, I lined up a better job to start in the fall when I got back to school, a very sweet gig at Harvard Business School fixing computers. I was able to save up those ten Gs so I wouldn't starve to death when I inevitably took a huge pay cut to break into news. I wasn't going to get caught short again. I'd learned to keep my pockets lined, and that I could line them on my own, anywhere, anytime, in a hurry.

That's power, baby.

That power was a feeling my mother never really had a chance to experience for herself. Maybe she got a vicarious taste through my sister and me. But she used money to control us—our comings and goings, our getting and spending, our wildest dreams. She kept the checkbook, so she ran the show, and I vowed I would never be in that type of relationship again, beholden to someone else for money. And yes, I do see the irony that those paychecks in reality had my name on them. But unlike most child actors who blame their parents for spending the money they earned, I do believe my mother was entitled to a good percentage of that pay.

And who cares about that long-gone cash anyway? I for one definitely do not. The money may have been spent as quickly as the checks came in, but I learned a lot about money during those years, more than most people learn in their entire lives. The fact that I then went on to study economics at Harvard and made a career as a financial reporter is no coincidence. As Freud would say, there are no accidents. Perhaps as a result of these formative experiences, I have an undeniable need to work and earn. I can't remember a single time in my life when I haven't had some sort of paycheck coming in. And I feel anxious if I'm not working full-time on someone's weekly payroll; I have a hard time sleeping at night. The more sources of income the better.

That drive has fostered a Protestant work ethic that has served me well and endeared me to employers. My husband has the same core ethic in spades, and our kids can't help but notice how hard we each work. Just in case they miss it, I'm certain to make the point when they want another five-million-dollar Lego, or they waste an Eggo at breakfast. I'm quick to remind them how hard their parents work (they inevitably look sad and guilty, and I feel I've gone too far. Ah, the joys of parenting).

But while I'm nagging, here's what I will tell them (a thousand times before they turn eighteen and run screaming from my house):

First, like it or not, money is power, and knowing you can make money on your own is powerful. And liberating. My mother never had an independent job outside our home in my lifetime. She often said that she thought no one would pay her on her own. I don't believe that for one second, but she did, and that belief trapped and controlled her. I know I'm employable. I will make sure my daughter cherishes and nurtures her own ability to support herself, even if she chooses to stay home with her family. She'll know if she decides to say home and do the hard work of raising her children full-time, she's made a choice that she can reverse if necessary, and jump back into the workforce in a flash. She won't be beholden to anyone for money to survive. And let me be perfectly clear, my sons will understand the same message. They will also understand that work and paychecks and caretaking for that matter have no gender.

Second, you are an idiot if you spend money like today's paycheck will be your paycheck every week for the rest of your life. This one might seem a little obvious, but fortunes rise and fall. Plan ahead. Save for a rainy day—or a monsoon. I promise you bad weather is in the forecast. Have the funds to wait out the storm indoors, in comfort.

Most wealthy people I've covered in the news business hate spending their own money. The key to accumulating is not spending. Duh! Michael Landon didn't spend a dime unless he had to, and much like him, I hate wasting money. I work really hard. Don't get me wrong: I love a good bag just as much as the next girl. But how many do you need? Wastefulness doesn't make you look rich, just stupid.

Third, being wealthy means the ability to meet your monthly nut, whether that obligation is $10 or $10 million, without stressing. The cliché is correct, money can't buy you happiness, but not being able to pay your mortgage really makes you cranky and sick to your stomach.

"Rich" isn't a number, because "wealth" is relative and means something different to everyone. I tell my kids, no matter how much you have, or how little, there's always someone with more and someone with less. Always! The richest tycoon is envious of some guy who has a bigger yacht. And you can always count your blessings compared to some poor person who has less, sadly. So don't waste your time measuring your stack against your neighbor's. Know that you are rich if you can sleep at night without worrying about your bills—truly, that is the bottom line.

Fourth, every paycheck gets my respect. If you show up for work and do your job, good for you! To make the wheels of any industry turn, you need every ball and gear to be in place, working hard and working together. All jobs have dignity, and so do the people who work them. All workers deserve respect. If you put in an honest day's work, you should hold your head high, always proud of your contribution.

I know that much of these lessons have already sunk in with my children. In fact, my younger son, Greyson, likes to gather up abandoned and forgotten bits of toys around the apartment and try to sell them to strangers on the playground. Apparently he's secretly binging on old episodes of *Sanford and Son* when I'm at work.

He fills a box and makes a sign that says "Every-thing $1 or 50 Cents!" There's no rhyme, reason, or consistency to which is what price. Then he parks himself in the middle of the jungle gym. Initially at least, when he begins shouting "TOYS FOR SALE!" our New York City neighbors start looking at him as if he's either yet another local madman or just someone using toys as bait to trap them into buying life insur-ance. At this point (please do not tell Greyson) I've been known to hand a few quarters to curious kids to prime the pump and get the selling started (I've learned the hard way he's not going home without off-loading all his merchandise).

But I gotta love the kid: he gets a taste of a few quarters, and his selling goes into high gear. He won't stop until every half-chewed remote control missing an antenna has been pawned off on some curious four-year-old. And forget trying to return the remote control when you realize it controls nothing remotely. He says, "Buyer beware. Trade-ins only!" Though in fairness, he won't let a customer go away unhappy. He's no scoundrel. He always manages to dig up a tan-talizing replacement that leaves everyone feeling they made a good deal.

He originally set up shop the day my older son, Thompson, borrowed (without asking) our new neigh-bors' red wagon and sped off to the same set of mon-key bars to charge desperate parents a quarter to spin their toddlers around the perimeter of the playground.

He made good money that day. Turns out lots of parents were happy for the break Thompson was quite industriously providing, doing laps around the jungle gym for hours. Greyson saw the fat wad of cash his brother raked in that day and wasn't going to let Thompson dominate the Salesman of the Month board for long.

You may think that allowing my sons to shake down neighborhood kids for loose change is testing the boundaries of morality. Perhaps. But I learned the value of sweat equity at an early age. I'm quite pleased to see them grin as they roll up their sleeves and make change.

CHAPTER SIX

MODERN MIRACLE

E very time I opened my eyes, there was another person at my feet. Or was I imagining them? Popping up like worried elves in muted green scrubs. I'd been in labor for twenty-five hours, though I'd long ago lost track of time. I thought the elves' faces should look more hopeful. More congratulatory. I was doing what I thought was a really good job. I was much tougher than I'd imagined I was going to be in this moment. Fighting hard through the pain instead of strangling someone (my husband).

But when my son finally emerged, the worried elves whisked him away before I could get a good look. He was a bluish blur, a glistening knot of purple blood and slime. This wasn't the joyous scene I'd been promised, with the gorgeous newborn wrapped like a peapod, handed to the new parents, who weep with joy.

Instead, alarms screamed above tense voices shouting orders. The sprawling team rushed to a makeshift emergency area, trying to get our baby to breathe, as Wray trailed them. Then they insisted he back away, and the thundercloud of noise and concern rushed from the room and vanished. Like a puff of smoke. Leaving me alone with my husband, collapsed in a chair next to me, and one lone elf at my feet, quietly sewing.

The weight of the frantic sprint from the room suddenly broke through. I looked at my husband, slumped in the chair.

"Wray," I said. He didn't look up. He didn't hear me.

"Wray!"

He looked up.

"He's dead, isn't he?" I said quietly.

"I think so," Wray responded, looking through me.

I crumpled into tears. So much work, I thought. So much effort. So much pain and worry. For nothing! I had nothing. I'd take home nothing. Nothing. No baby, just emptiness.

I closed my eyes and let the tears flood through my lashes, puddling on the front of my hospital gown. I might have drowned, and no one would have noticed. I don't know how much time passed before one of the other elves dressed in scrubs returned.

"Your son is okay," he said. "He's in the NICU." I was surprised my son was alive. And skeptical. This person was lying.

"May I see him?" I asked.

"No," he said, predictably. "He can't leave the NICU, and you can't move. We are going to take you to another recovery room, but you can't sit up. Your blood pressure is very high. We don't want you to have a stroke, so you need to stay lying down. You need to try to rest while we work on your blood pressure."

"So I can't see my son?" I tried again.

"No, I'm sorry, not this second."

Yep, he was lying. *My son is dead,* I thought, *but they don't want to admit the truth because they're afraid the news will kill me too.* I looked at Wray, who asked a battery of logical questions related to nothing I cared about since I wasn't going to be allowed to see my son. I just wanted to sleep.

What a horrific waste this had all been.

We were married for seven and half years before we decided to have children. We knew instinctively that having a baby would toss a Molotov cocktail into the center of our pretty blissful lives. But I hadn't considered that coming up with another human being would be so difficult. After all, I'd gone to Catholic school, where the teachers impressed upon us from the start that the slightest wrong move could result in a child. Swim in a public pool, forget to wash your hands before lunch, who knows? You might get pregnant. We were taught that birth control would make God a bit angry, but

using the rhythm method was akin to playing Russian
roulette with a bullet in each and every chamber. Bottom line, accidental babies lurked around every corner.

Seems they were stretching the biological facts to
frighten us.

I'd gotten pregnant with my son Thompson the
first month we pulled the goalie (okay, so maybe the
nuns had a point), but I was so terrified about how
dramatically my life was about to change that I pro-
ceeded as if I'd just had an extra cheeseburger. Nothing to see here. We hardly told anyone, so I just rolled
along like the inevitable wasn't coming.

I couldn't fathom shifting to a slower gear at
work. I'd made a name for myself covering the energy
beat for CNBC at a time when no one wanted the assignment. Shortly after I took over coverage, a barrel
of crude oil went from nearly free to the price of a
small house, and suddenly I was on the air every other
minute. The *New York Post* dubbed me the "Empress of
Energy" because I was the first person to report live
on camera from the oil trading pits at the New York
Mercantile Exchange. I owned the beat, and I wasn't
giving up what I'd built. So Thompson's in utero pass-
port was stamped early and often: he chased down the
Saudi oil delegation at OPEC meetings in Vienna and
stood feet from Hugo Chavez in Caracas, with long
rifles pointed our way just in case we got feisty.

But at the very end of the pregnancy, something
went very wrong (See nuns? Not easy). My blood

pressure shot through the roof. The doctors forced me onto bed rest, but I'm not a good bed-rest kind of patient. You could duct-tape my lids closed, but I would still see all the things that needed to be washed, organized, and reorganized before the baby arrived. I'm not a very relaxed or relaxing person. Just ask our building super, who might one day respond to my nagging by accidentally spraying my toothbrush with pesticide so he can finally get some peace.

Finally, my doctor decided that Thompson was no longer thriving. She said I had preeclampsia, a fancy name for pregnant women who have temporarily high blood pressure. Mine was too high, and, as a result, Thompson's was too low.

Not to worry, my doctor said. They would induce. Sounded good to me. I was ready to get this show on the road. I was cooked. But, turns out, Thompson was not, and there was plenty to worry about when he came out of the oven way too early.

He spent the first eleven days of his life in the Neonatal Intensive Care Unit. For the first forty-eight hours I wasn't even allowed to see him. Can you imagine giving birth to a child you weren't allowed to see? Except in one fleeting moment when he was rushed from the room in a blur of screaming sirens?

But I couldn't be moved. He couldn't be moved. Too dangerous for both of us, the doctors said. I kept mentioning my suspicion that Thompson was dead. So Wray used his phone to take a photo of Thompson in the NICU and brought the image to me to prove my son was alive.

Bless Wray's heart, that made everything a thousand times worse.

Thompson was riddled with tubes. Wires stuck into his translucent skin, and he wore a tiny, pathetic helmet. He looked more like a broken baby bird that had fallen from the nest than a human being.

I convulsed with deep sobs, looking at my poor, fragile bird. This disaster was entirely my fault for not slowing down. I should have done every single thing differently. I had no idea how I was going to live with myself after causing this.

A woman walked into my room who I assumed was yet another nurse stopping by so I could fail yet another test. She asked me how I was feeling. I muttered something incoherent. Two or three incredibly stupid questions floated by before she asked, "Do you think you are excessively worried about your son's health?"

Excessively?

I hadn't seen my son since I gave birth to him and an emergency swat team swept him out of the room in a full-force panic. I had completely failed as a mother before I had even held my only child once. I still hadn't held him or even seen him in person. What's the maximum amount of worried and destroyed that a human could be? That level wasn't excessive enough. She was probing to see if I had postpartum depression? How about the fact that my world was imploding and I'd been the cause?

Holy insult to injury.

"Please leave me alone," I said. "Please get out."

The social worker asked if I thought I might hurt myself.

"How much more hurt could I possibly get?"

On the third day, I was finally wheeled down the hall to see my tiny bird. He was fighting like mad, ripping the wires from his spindly arms, tearing off his miniature helmet that wouldn't have fit a doll. And he appeared to be screaming, though the volume didn't amount to anything audible (yet).

He was feisty.

I was only allowed to remove him from his clear incubator in very small doses. The rest of the time, I could only peer at him through a plastic wall. I watched helplessly as Thompson screamed and cried and flailed wildly, burning energy he couldn't spare. I wanted to swaddle him and hold him the way I'd been taught. But instead the NICU nurses insisted he stay naked in his sterile incubator. He shrunk down to four pounds as he wasted precious calories fighting. And as he shrunk, I made promises through the plastic, vowing that when he was free from his little cage, I would hold him and love him and never set him down.

And that's how I turned him into my own personal grenade.

See, all babies would like to be held twenty-four hours a day. Which is what I did the minute we left the hospital, both of us licking our wounds and recovering from his bruising entry into the world. I was going to make up for lost time, and Thompson loved to snuggle. And why not? I was soft and warm. Newborn Thompson slept like an angel in my arms, and if I set him down to, say, assemble food for myself, or take a shower—well, then he would start screaming his little lungs out. I'd already let him down so tremendously. I wouldn't fail again. So I held him. Around the clock.

Jedi knight of babies I was not.

--=◎ ◎=--

Of course, this was a terrible strategy. Ask anyone who has ever cared for an infant. Or try carrying a five-pound weight around in both your arms like a loaf of bread, and tell me how easy it is to brush your teeth. Now walk up and down the hall with the little loaf of lead. At 3:00 a.m. Not ideal, right?

Spent, Wray and I hired professionals to come in and undo what I'd done. And, one by one, they fled in the night, exhausted to the point of tears by our tiny terror who had figured out how to keep the adults of the world from setting him down, at all, ever, for any reason. Who was the master of Jedi mind tricks now? He was a feisty baby after all he'd been through. He had us all by the tail, and he was little more than a minute old. He wore a satisfied little grin when we did what he wanted. And I smiled too, though I still couldn't manage to pry him loose so I could at least apply more deodorant.

When I called the mystified nanny agency yet again to explain that yet another of their nurses had run screaming from our home before dawn, the manager said he had one last idea, a woman they called the Baby Whisperer. He explained that Ms. Whisperer wouldn't wash bottles, do laundry, or paint our apartment. She had only one mission: sleep.

I didn't even ask her hourly rate. I just hung up the phone and walked directly to the front door to stand by and wait patiently for our savior to arrive.

Later that day, Ann floated through the door, set down her bag, and took one look at the snoring infant in my arms before announcing rather boldly that I was the problem. (Hey look at me! I suck at being a mom again!) She explained that he needed to learn to sleep on his own (fat chance, lady). Then she pried Tiny Thompson from my arms and set him down in his crib, where instantly, his eyes popped open, and his deceptively small mouth exploded into screams that could shatter windows in the next state.

And as he screamed bloody murder, she swept him back up in her arms and performed what appeared to be a ritualistic jungle dance, the motion of which supposedly mimicked the jostling that occurs in utero. She hopped from foot to foot while swinging her upper body from left to right simultaneously. We would come to call this The Bad Eighties Dance.

As she hopped, I mentally began redialing the phone to find a sane baby nurse. Then Thompson's eardrum bursting wails fell completely silent. From a ten plus to zero faster than you can say, "This is all your fault, Melissa!"

She had knocked him out with really terrible dancing.

She was hired.

And with that, I finally had a moment to reflect.

And go to the bathroom alone.

"I'm not totally convinced they figured out what was wrong with you," Wray said, breaking the blessed silence. "I mean, what went wrong, in the end, with the delivery. At the hospital. Or the pregnancy. Or why everything went so far south."

"Doctors really don't know anything," I said, sharing my most frightening (and accurate) analysis on doctors, which has yet to be proven wrong. "They just identify the most likely cause for whatever your symptom is, and if that's not it and you aren't the norm, you're super-duper screwed."

⇥≡◎≡⇤

Three years later, Thompson was thriving. He was enormous for his age. We'd almost forgotten the trial we'd been through, and we got brave (stupid) enough to try again.

But this time, my blood pressure shot through the roof immediately.

"I think we misdiagnosed what happened last time," my doctor said. Now she wasn't sure I'd ever had preeclampsia (here's that whole thing about the most likely explanation not always being the correct explanation and the outlier being super-duper screwed).

Now she wanted me to see a specialist, one of the leading researchers in this area. Wray had been right. No one in the hospital had correctly identified what the hell went so very wrong with Thompson.

Instead, what was wrong with me was a very rare genetic mutation, an abnormality. (Yes! My fault again! Obviously. I was getting used to this.) I had a hereditary condition known as Factor V Leiden, which causes blood clots in less than 5 percent of white people of European descent. In other words, I was one of a very, very select few—not exactly the sort of exclusive club anyone fought to join. That's why no one thought to check for the condition. In most cases, the blood disorder simply lies dormant, but combined with risk factors like smoking and pregnancy, this mutation could easily cause a blood clot or a stroke. Not surprisingly, a number of people in my family tree had died of strokes. Now we knew why.

I was only six or seven weeks into the pregnancy. The doctor said if I wanted to keep the baby and not

terminate or have a miscarriage, I would need to in-
ject myself with blood thinner multiple times a day—
at home, at work, throughout the pregnancy, and for
months afterwards.

I'd always been squeamish about needles and
blood. I got woozy and nauseous the first hundred or
so times I pierced my own skin and watched the liquid
inside the barrel of the needle penetrate my skin and
then form a mountain underneath my flesh at the in-
jection site before dispersing. I was covered in bruises
and welts, and running out of fresh patches of skin to
pierce. And the whole time I was pregnant, I felt my
pulse pound in my throat and threaten to strangle me,
as my thickened blood throbbed and forced its way
slowly through my veins.

I felt I was dying all the time.

⊷⊷●◐⊷⊷

When I finally gave birth to our second son, Greyson,
the experience was wildly different from Thompson's
birth. Greyson was even smaller than his brother,
barely tipping the scales at four pounds at birth. But
he was perfectly serene. I swear he wore a smile when
they wrapped him in the thin hospital blanket and
handed him to his father. I loved his tiny perfection,
but I was spent.

They had gutted me like a tuna while I was awake
to deliver him (not pleasant). And once they sewed my

stomach and liver and other important parts back inside (with me listening), the nurse asked if she could get me anything.

Greyson was snuggling with his father, so I asked, "Can I see my older son?" In my weakened, debilitated state, I felt I'd neglected Thompson for almost ten months of his three years on Earth. But again, I wasn't allowed to see Thompson. Just like before. That was infuriating, but I was helpless. I just wanted to be wheeled into a closet (with my important organs), with the lights out and the door closed behind me, to recover.

Like his brother, Greyson went to the NICU but to a part of the unit we called the Halfway House. He didn't need any special attention in spite of his premature status and low birth weight. He had a voracious appetite, and other than that, he was content to snooze. He bulked up in no time. But I wasn't healthy enough to care for him immediately, so he was fussed over by a team of nurses and his thrilled father, while I healed down the hall. Again.

Somewhere in there, my doctor made a pronouncement. I could not have any more children, she said. The risk of having a stroke or a blood clot in my lungs was way too high. And in case I was tempted to ignore her, she put the severity of the risk to me in no uncertain terms. She said, "Please rehearse the speech your husband will tell the boys about why they weren't enough for you and you died trying to have a third child."

Harsh.

But that's the type of thing you need to say to a woman who thinks rules and limits are for other, weaker people. Just as I'd volunteered to go on assignment to North Korea, a hostile nation with Third World medical care, a month before I was due with Thompson, I was not to be trusted to make sound medical decisions.

I told Wray about my conversation with the doctor and held my breath, knowing that he wanted more children very much.

"Oh my goodness, no!" he cried. "I would NEVER want you to risk your life, or go through this, ever again. This has been way too hard on you. I love you. We couldn't risk you!"

Then, a throwaway line:

"Besides, there are much easier ways for us to have more children."

I'm sorry, what?

Now, I went to fifth grade. That's the place Mrs. Miller led the obligatory and completely uncomfortable illustrated tour of the human body. In sixth grade, Mrs. Phillips went one step further and turned out the lights to show us the cryptically scientific film *Where Babies Come From*. Think back to the film I'm describing.

It wasn't, like, multiple choice.

There didn't appear to be easy, medium, and extra-hard ways for the mom and dad in the film to have a baby. There was pretty much one.

But back to my loving husband, Wray, and his assertion that we were clearly doing things the hard way. We had two awesome boys. Frick and Frack, Mutt and Jeff, Loud and Louder, whatever we called them on a given day, they hadn't been easy to come by. I was happy to be alive. The Squabble Twins were healthy, and so was I. Whew! We had a family of four! We could sit at a square table. Fit in one cab. Use man on man defense, one parent per kid, no need for the zone.

Done and done.

Greyson was getting big and strong and adventurous. One morning I heard a huge thwack followed by air-siren wails. I ran to his bedroom and found him wide-eyed and panicked on the floor, screaming. He'd scrambled over the top of his crib and plummeted to the floor below.

Time to buy him a real bed.

I ordered adorable wooden bunk beds for Greyson's room. New York apartments are so small, you have to use all the available space in all three dimensions. That can mean expanding up toward the ceiling. Bunk beds meant sleepovers. Fun!

The moment Thompson saw the beds, he grabbed his stuffed animal, his pillow, and his flashlight and abandoned his own room next door. The bunks looked too much like a jungle gym to resist. The boys were already close. Now they moved in together. They'd horse trade over who slept on top and who slept on the bottom, and then end up in the same bed often times, snuggled together. They might complain that someone was snoring, but no one was ever willing to sleep elsewhere.

Before too long, I caught Wray staring into Thompson's now abandoned room, which had turned into our own Museum of Abandoned Toys. I knew exactly what he was thinking.

There are much easier ways for us to have more children.

I tried to pretend I hadn't heard him say that particular, somewhat ludicrous sentence. That was kooky talk. But I could see the line lingering in the air, floating above his head in a cartoon word bubble, as he eyed the Legos in Thompson's old room gathering dust.

⊷⊜ ⊜⊷

One thing it helps to know about Wray is that the distance between my husband and what he wants is just logistics. That is the essential truth I have learned about him. So I wasn't the least bit surprised when he made the appointment to meet with Melissa Brisman, a lawyer who specialized in surrogacy. We were supposed to be at her offices in New Jersey at eight o'clock one weekday morning. I had shoehorned-in the appointment before my shows that day.

I thought what we were doing was completely insane. We had gone insane. That was the only explanation. And at some point during the drive over George Washington Bridge, I was sure Wray was going to pull the plug, pop a U-turn, and announce that he was just kidding when he suggested piling even more on top of our larger-than-life lives.

Instead he kept driving to Paramus.

The sign on Melissa Brisman's door said "Reproductive Possibilities." That was certainly one way to put it.

Most of the literature inside her office seemed to be targeted at same-sex couples. In fact, we'd met a number of same-sex couples in Manhattan with surrogate children. Thompson's favorite playmate when he was a toddler had two dads. She wasn't adopted, her nanny had explained, unsolicited. Her dads eventually had three children, and from the family pictures I could tell they were all genetically related—but which child to which dad, I'd never be rude enough to ask (even though the curious reporter in me was dying to know).

At the Catholic school the boys now attended, I knew of another family with surrogate children. I'd heard they had a long and painful journey with fertility treatments before deciding to go the surrogacy route. Clearly, we would have plenty of company in this choice if we indeed went down this road.

I listened to how the whole process would work, and the feeling that we were completely insane grew. First we'd head to the fertility doctor to harvest my eggs—if we chose to use them and if my body cooperated. That could take months. And many more injections! Perrrrrrrrrfect. Then, on to meeting women who might be willing to do this Herculean thing for us. If we all felt comfortable with each other, there'd be medical tests. Finally, if we cleared all those hurdles, the doctor would transfer our embryo into this other person, who would carry around my child inside her body for the better part of a year before handing him or her back over to us forever.

I listened to Brisman's speech and tried not to have any sort of expression on my face at all. A therapist once told me that when I get scared or panicked, I hold completely still and try to wipe my face clean of all emotion. My "tell" is sort of the anti-tell. So by trying not to give away anything, I give away the farm. At this moment, I looked blank and frozen in time.

Suddenly, Brisman stopped and asked if we had any questions. I didn't even know where to start. So I just slowly turned my eyes to Wray.

I can't remember what he asked; I'm sure his queries were thoughtful. As for me, I kept honestly waiting for someone to ask why we were being so selfish, so greedy. Why we weren't grateful for what we already had. Satisfied. After all, we had two healthy children. Strong, beautiful sons. I was fine as the only girl in our family. More than fine. My relationship with my mother was such a source of pain and self-doubt, I wasn't sure I could mother a daughter. I just figured that God through his grace had decided I would have boys. I should have thought better than to guess at God's intentions.

Meanwhile, Wray was enthusiastic. He's a born problem solver. The original can-do guy. A delightfully charming, turbo-powered steamroller. My blood condition was just another bump in the road he'd smooth and flatten into a highway that carried us forward.

But just how easy this easier way was remained to be seen.

Harvesting eggs isn't simple. But the first real surprise came shortly after that, when the doctor told us the embryos were exclusively girls. There would be no gender selection for us. The idea of choosing the sex of a child makes many people uncomfortable, angry, outraged—furious, even. We didn't have to worry about offending anyone on that front at least. Our baby would be a girl, or I would have to keep on harvesting, and let me tell you I was ready to hang up my rake and hoe.

Armed with embryos that needed a welcoming host, Brisman's office sent us a profile of a woman from another state willing to help our family. But after months of getting to know each other, background checks, flights for her up to New York and back, and a fleet of medical tests, she failed a basic drug screening.

Wray and I stared at each other in shock.

"How could she put us through all that?" I mused. "All that time and effort and emotion and energy on all our parts, and then to go off and smoke pot. She had to know it would show up in the drug screening." The action was insane. And on this woman's questionnaire she had sworn she had never even tried marijuana.

I wondered if this was a sign. Wray was undeterred (big surprise).

Brisman's office sent us more candidate files to consider. Now we had a hard time knowing what to look for, or trusting ourselves or the faces in the files.

Finally, I opened a manila folder, and there they were. A family of four beaming right back at me. A stunning, glowing couple, with his-and-her heads of dark, shining hair so glossy the strands looked blue in the photo, and two very young daughters blended from their parents' perfect features. The entire family was dressed in active wear, out playing in the sunshine. I thought they might jump out of the file and run a quick marathon just for fun.

There was no doubt this was our family, if they'd have us.

Briana and Trenton had started their family at a young age. Briana described her pregnancies and deliveries as "easy." That word made me laugh. What a different experience we'd had.

The questionnaire asked why Briana was willing to do this. I was almost afraid to read that part. She said she simply wanted to help another family.

Now, you're reading this and thinking this family was financially motivated. I don't blame you. I made that mistake too, at first. And to be sure, some women who volunteer for this superhuman sacrifice are moved to do so out of financial need—and there's nothing wrong with that, in my humble opinion. Nurses get paid to help people every day; that compensation doesn't make their work any less heroic. But in the months that followed our first meeting, and all during the pregnancy, any time I tried to pay for something or sent Briana or her family a gift, she was clearly insulted. Remember, my daughter was wedged in between her vital organs. My baby was kicking her in the stomach as she ate, while also sitting on her bladder. The least I could do was pay for her lunch when we saw her. But she bristled every time.

How could there be such a generous, selfless person? Briana had started down this path when she volunteered to carry a baby for a relative, who ultimately changed her mind. Then the doctor suggested there were many, many other families who were desperate for the same help, if she was still willing. Briana had heard the call and wanted to help. The choice was that simple to her.

She came to visit us in New York, met our sons, and got to know us. We introduced her to Thompson and Greyson simply as our friend, and they were instantly all over her like white on rice. They could smell a kid expert from a mile away. In addition to raising her daughters, she spent every weekday assistant-teaching a class of third graders (experience she needed to earn her teaching degree). She also spent part of the weekends waiting tables on the side, to pay for her education.

She and Trenton worked, went to school, raised a family, all at once.

"How in the world do you have the time and the energy for all that?" I asked.

She shrugged as if it were no big deal.

"We figure, when the girls go off to college, we'll still be in our thirties," she started to explain.

"Thirties?" I choked.

When I gave birth to my sons, I was in my thirties. Her daughters would be leaving home. When my kids leave for college, I just hope to still have my original teeth and hips.

"At that point," she continued, "we'll have our whole lives ahead of us. We can relax, travel, whatever."

What a thought.

Like so many women around me, I'd been raised with very focused marching orders. Get your education first. Boys later. Start climbing that ladder, fast-fast-fast, and scramble up at least half a dozen rungs. Then (and only then) should you start to think about marriage. And kids? There's plenty of time for them later. Plenty!

Except there isn't. Women see the glossy-glam photos of Hollywood actresses having babies in their forties and even a few in their fifties (Janet Jackson!), and they think that's a real possibility. They believe the snapshot. The magazine headline screams: "They're Just Like Us!" They don't notice the fingerprints of modern science all over those pictures; they've been Photoshopped right out—along with the miscarriages and fertility treatments and heartbreak. We never hear if those celebrities were able to use their own eggs or how many tried a dozen times before giving up, completely devastated.

But what if "modern" women like me have been subscribing to the wrong Order of Things? The "Princeton Mom," Susan Patton, stirred up a shizzle-storm of controversy when she had the nerve to suggest that women (and men) who left college without locking down a life partner were fools. Her thinking was basic: When are you ever going to be exposed to such a wide array of potential partners, with similar interests, who are age appropriate and have similar goals and values? Patton was promptly fitted with a metal skewer and roasted.

But I wonder how wrong her thesis really is—no matter how much, as modern women, we hated hearing the news.

In high school and college, I was firmly in the camp that I was never getting married. I couldn't imagine the upside. I didn't babysit; I didn't particularly like or understand babies. I mean, you seriously cannot reason with them; they seem to just do whatever moves them. Plus, my own mother always struck me as completely miserable and horribly trapped. She was the first to tell me to avoid her mistakes. I knew I could always support myself. I'd brought home a paycheck since I was six months old. I didn't need a husband to pay the bills, certainly. Why not a boyfriend whom you could return to the dealer when you tired of him, and trade in for a fresh model?

I got very lucky when one of my best friends, Nicole, reintroduced me to my future husband. Wray had been my next-door neighbor in the dorm at Harvard, and I'd stopped by to flirt with him many times, though he didn't seem to notice (note to Wray: you still haven't properly explained that, my friend). My flirting amounted to nothing; Wray graduated and went on his way. While I was moving around New England from one reporter job to another, I came down to visit Nicole, and she "introduced" me to a guy who turned out to be Wray. He had the nerve to not immediately remember our connection.

How in the world did he manage to recover from this series of insults? The short answer is tequila. But the lasting answer is this: he's wildly exciting and perfectly calm at the same time. Who can make your pulse race and your blood pressure drop at once? I knew I'd never find that combination again.

But I certainly had many friends who weren't as lucky, who put off marriage and family until the field of potential mates narrowed to slim pickins or their fertility evaporated. At the very least, I was rethinking the guidance about in what order to erect the big tent poles of your life that I would share with the daughter Briana was carrying.

⊷⊷ ⊷⊷

When Briana hit thirty-nine weeks, we packed up our crazy crew and flew to Phoenix to witness the birth of our daughter and bring her home. The boys were bouncing off the walls to meet their new sister. They had wanted a puppy, but we were doing them one better!

They kept telling people they were about to get a new baby sister, and the unsuspecting person's eyes would travel to my mid-section slowly, and then they would say something like, "Does your Mommy know that?" In fact, in the months leading up to this day, Greyson's teachers listened to him describe his impending joy and just assumed he had a vivid imagination. Now he was proving he was no nut.

We ended up baking in the July heat in Phoenix for two full weeks, waiting for our daughter to arrive. We'd thought Briana's water might break at thirty-nine weeks, just like with her own daughters. Fourteen days after that, we were still waiting and boiling in the desert.

We saw every single museum, park, zoo, natural attraction, teepee, and family bathroom Arizona had to offer during that stretch. At one outpost, the ranger had the nerve to say, "Thank goodness it's not hot!"

I gave him a look that would melt ice, if only ice could exist in this broiling corner of hell.

"Usually this time of year, the thermometer tops 120 degrees. Today it's only 112!" He smiled coolly.

I'm not sure we would have noticed the difference.

The upside was that we got the tans of a lifetime. And our boys were delighted to spend as much time as possible with Trenton and Briana's brilliant little girls, Bella and Ayvah. Plus, the totally bizarre nature of what we were doing had forced intimacy before we had a chance to really know each other. But this time made the bond real.

At forty-one weeks, the doctors finally set a time to induce poor Briana, who had incredibly high spirits for someone who was a week overdue in the middle of summer. I would have been a fire-breathing dragon by that point. Amazingly, she had the strength to bring her family to a twenty-acre water park with us the day before she gave birth. After three hours of trying not to swallow the chemically treated water or faint from heat stroke, I'd had enough, so I announced I was taking my family back to our hotel to get some rest before the big day.

Briana said her team had another twenty slides in them, so they stayed until the sun disappeared into the desert sand. Amazing.

⊷⊨◉ ◉⊨⊷

When the time came, Wray, Trenton, and I stood by in the delivery room while Briana pushed. In many ways, I think I had the dad experience this time around. Watching someone else go through so much pain and effort and intensity, while I stood by hopeful and helpless, was humbling. I would have done anything to take a fraction of the burden or the pain from Briana, but of course that was totally impossible.

When our daughter emerged, all four of us wept with joy. We decided to call her Gemma, our Little Gem.

Through tears, Trenton said, "Thank you for taking us on your journey," as Briana nodded, beyond words.

We were floored.

Let that sink in for a moment.

They thanked *us* for taking *them* on the journey.

Later Wray said, "I feel like the worst person in the world—to watch someone else go through so much for us . . . " His voice broke. I just shook my head with tears rolling down my cheeks as well. The gratitude and wonder overwhelmed us. I still cry thinking about the gift.

A day later, both families crowded into the same room and took turns passing Gemma around, laughing loudly, cooing at her while she slept, oblivious to the noise. We took photos with every combination of mothers, daughters, brothers, sisters, and dads. Finally we all squeezed in for the photo I will cherish for the rest of my life: Gemma surrounded by all the people who had made her little life possible.

We shared a copy of that extraordinary photo with the group of nurses and doctors and caregivers of every sort at Banner Desert Medical Center whom we will never forget. Senior nurse Kathleen Chittenden led the team, enveloping us with a warm cloud of support. Our experience wasn't the first time she navigated the murky waters of one couple giving birth to a child for another family. What's the protocol around that? Can you imagine such a scene? What's right and wrong? Who decides? Kathie certainly had more answers than we did, but more essential, she was brave and gentle enough to lead the expedition into this brand new territory.

One of the great blessings of the experience—other than Gemma herself, of course—was watching the whole story unfold through the eyes of Gemma's brothers. (Fun fact: I caught their highly detailed questions about the science behind this miracle on camera—to be saved for eternity and shown at each of their wedding rehearsal dinners for laughs.) They are kids, after all, so they had no sense of propriety or why any of this would be awkward. They just rolled around in the joy, smearing themselves with happiness.

Thompson went back to school in the fall, and one of his first assignments in his third-grade class was to draw a picture of a hero in his life. There were loads of Batmans, firefighters, moms, and one Darth Vader that may have attracted the attention of the school counselor. Thompson drew a picture of Briana, and underneath the sketch he wrote: "Because she had my baby sister."

I was certainly glad I had tissues in my purse at back-to-school night when I sat down at Thompson's little desk and found the drawing. He hadn't mentioned the assignment to me. I used my phone to take a photo, and then I sent the snapshot to Briana, so she'd know how grateful he was, thousands of miles away, just thinking about her on his own.

Okay, go ahead. Hit me with your best questions. Everyone else has. A driver shuttling me between the hospital and our hotel in Phoenix asked me if we'd used my egg or someone else's. I thought about asking him if he was circumcised, in return.

But seriously . . .

I know some people wonder, Can a mother love a child she didn't carry as much as she loves the boys she birthed? Is it the same? Very close friends have summoned the courage to ask me directly (usually with the help of a few glasses of wine). How many people can answer that question? I will save you the trouble of asking. Every day, I look into my daughter's stunningly bright blue eyes, speckled with white flecks that make them look like fresh-cut crystal, and just laugh. Of course I love her the very same amount as the boys, which is to the moon and back. Deeper than any ocean.

Is it wrong that we used genetics, modern medicine—weird science, to some—to add to a family that was already blessed with two healthy children? Were we selfish and greedy? Ungodly?

If you think so.

One more lesson perhaps is to take a risk, take a wild leap, especially if it's your chance to love *more*. You might be surprised by the heroes you meet on the way, who you never would have believed existed. You might even start believing in miracles.

But don't take my word for any of it. I'll let you look at the photos, the pure joy that is our now extended family, and be the judge.

Chapter Seven

Show Them Your Cellulite

I t always struck me as funny, the amount of artifice that went into making *Little House* authentic. The show was based on actual humans who ventured out alone in a single, covered wagon, hunted by wolves and hostile Natives, eating anything they could find, clinging to each other for warmth and survival. These people were as real as they come.

But to replicate the desolate, amber fields of America's lonely prairie, several hundred buzzing perfectionists hauled a thousand tons of modern machines into the dust just off Southern California's 118 Freeway, as far from Kansas and Minnesota as we could be. To achieve their bare, sun-scorched complexion, we layered on an inch and a half of pumpkin-colored base. And because these pioneers could only afford one single dress, we packed three dozen replicas of that frock to wear again and again and again.

We moved mountains of fraud to try to achieve the truth.

That's a lot of effort. To make a hit television show that brought in advertising dollars hand over fist, the end justified the means. But in my own life, especially as I get older, I can't justify going to such lengths to obfuscate the truth of anything, no matter how potentially humbling: cellulite, the birthdate on my driver's license, mistakes I make in front of the camera or in the privacy of my behind-the-scenes life. I've reached a point where I'm just too worn out to put up a good front. It's not worth it. I'm fine with who I am, take it or leave it. I've let down my guard, and boy, is that a relief.

"You're so sharp and fun and . . . funny! . . . in real life. You always make everyone at dinner laugh. Why don't you show more of that on television? Like when you do your show? I think viewers would love that Melissa. That's the real you. I don't see that Melissa so much when you're on TV. But what do I know?"

Words of wisdom from my husband that were totally annoying. I would call that a backhanded compliment if he weren't my loving husband. But this is a man who knows how to deliver constructive criticism. For example, instead of saying, "My God! Your ass looks HUUUUGE in that dress!" he would say something suave like, "My God! I love that dress! But you know which one looks even better? . . ."

You see what he did there? Same thing. He was trying to get me to wear a different personality on the air. Since the dawn of time, we anchormen and anchor ladies have behaved exactly the same way, hermetically sealed in plastic when in front of a camera, so no emotion, no opinion, none of our true essence accidentally seeped out into the real world. Showing a glimmer of our real self was letting our underwear show, and as I learned in elementary school (doing a cartwheel in my favorite yellow dress), that's no good.

I knew the TV persona was silly. Ron Burgundy made that point loud and clear. But that's how we did it, dammit!

I had failed to notice that those clever viewers had begun clicking away from stiff-blazer-wearing men (and women) who read the news in fake voices three octaves below any normal human voice. They'd decided that old-school news façade set up a barrier, created distance. Suddenly they wanted talent who reached through the set and grabbed them by the shirt instead.

Sure, in the rearview, I should have seen the trend coming like a herd of water buffalo. Elsewhere in TV land, reality shows were wiping the floor with scripted television, and the friends I had from college who were writing smart-aleck jokes in Hollywood for sitcoms thought they might never work again. Everyone wanted what was real. Even within "reality," the American public wasn't buying the set-up stunts. (Who remembers *My Big, Fat, Obnoxious Fiancé?*)

Alas, like so many of my comrades in Aquanet hairspray, I was late to wake up and smell the coffee— probably because of all the hairspray fumes. All we really had to do was look to the Holy Roman Empress of Television, Oprah Winfrey.

She started out in Baltimore with huge shoulder pads reading the prompter just like the rest of us. Then she made the mystical transformation to what every man, woman, and child who has ever held a mic-flag dreams of: Megawatt Superstar Who Picks Our Presidents, Our Heroes, and Our Underwear (don't forget: she introduced us to Spanx). But why her? thousands of tearful pageant queens and valedictorians alike have asked.

People at home loved her the moment she got that show that bared her handwritten moniker because she was never some perfect, phony television personality. She just let it all hang out—in the most dignified way possible of course. She didn't dress up or mince words about her life, her weight, her struggles, her upbringing, her friendships . . . or her opinions. She was real, like it or not.

Okay, so with a nudge from Wray, I got the picture. But breaking that hermetic seal was another thing. There's no way to show just a touch of cellulite. Once that stuff hits the fresh air, you're exposed.

I started by conveniently leaving off the disclaimers. To me this felt like a little baby pinky toe in the water. You know how some people hedge and pepper their reports with qualifiers like the often-used "some say this, while others say that," or concluding with generic, placeholder observations like "only time will tell!" and throw up their arms in a questioning motion, like, "Who am I to judge?"

Well, you know what? I'll tell you who the hell I am to judge! This isn't my first rodeo, and in many cases, any clown can connect the dots. Like the time, before I came to Fox, when I got slapped on the wrist for suggesting the math didn't work with Obamacare. I wondered how it would be possible that more people would sign up for insurance, they would not be charged for expensive, preexisting conditions, and then somehow, magically everyone's costs would go down. Add more people who pay the same but use a ton of services? Either costs go up for everyone, or doctors do the work for free, right? More stuff costs more, no?

Yet when I questioned the math, I was told I was disrespecting the Office of the President. In other words: shut up, Melissa. Just report what he said. And shut your pie hole.

How's that a service to viewers? Why not say, "Let's be honest. We're all going to pay more to cover everyone, but perhaps as a society the outcome is worth the price. Or not! Let's discuss. But let's not go forward based on a lie that defies all logic and middle-school math."

But at that news shop, connecting the dots was strictly forbidden (perhaps depending on the result-ing picture). I was sent to the principal's office, but the genie was out of my bottle. I couldn't go back to hiding my thoughts and holding the audience at arm's length.

I know what you're thinking. "What's the big deal with that?" And you're right. Hosts like Rachel Mad-dow and Sean Hannity wield opinion like a torch, burning up the dial and scorching TV sets across the country. The hosts who really crush the ratings get their audience frothing at the mouth, and trust me they are as sold on what they're saying as the viewer, because with high-definition TV, I've got as much luck hiding a zit as a lie.

Ironically, not being me is exactly why I'd ditched acting. I was tired of pretending to be someone else on television, mouthing someone else's words, displaying someone else's emotions. I'd wanted to be myself—and this was my chance.

As I look back now at the way the business was turned on its head, Jon Stewart might have been the most clever pioneer at the forefront of the flip. What a genius! To do news with a decided point of view and clear agenda but hide the whole thing inside a big ball of brilliantly hilarious comedy. Broccoli so dripping in chocolate you have no idea there are any determined little vitamins underneath all that deliciousness working their way into your bloodstream. Entertain the viewers, and then slide the message down their throat while their mouths are wide open, laughing.

But here's the real truth that bears repeating: *Every news person has an opinion, a point of view.* If they don't, they aren't engaged in the subject, the news—and if they aren't engaged, filled with passion and rage, they don't belong in news anyway. Why do a show if you don't care? Why cover a topic if it bores you to sleep? Why would the audience care if you don't?

All news people who pretend to be unbiased are either bored to death with what they're doing or lying.

So why bother pretending to be neutral? Viewers can smell a phony through the television, and they don't want to be lied to any longer. Taken for stupid. That's why the nightly network news is tanking. No one wants to watch a phony. Things were only made worse by Brian Williams (sorry, Brian). His penchant for a tall tale put the death knell in the stiff-as-cardboard Walter Cronkite knockoffs. I know: I was one.

It's like going to see a doctor who refuses to answer the question, "What would you do if this were you?" Doctors who give the pros and cons of your health care options without weighing in on what they'd do if the tables were turned aren't very helpful, are they? As a patient, you come away from the appointment feeling like you don't matter enough to your doctor for her to be honest.

I can be honest enough to admit that where I come from and where I've been colors my point of view. I'm human. I have traveled on assignment to the Kingdom of Saudi Arabia more than once and had men speed by in cars screaming "Go home, American whore!" even though I was wearing an abaya and a headscarf (and they didn't even know me in college). I also spent enough time behind the scenes covering the Saudi oil minister and his entourage to know they are humans just like me with children and hilarious senses of humor and a ton of values I agree with and a mountain I don't. I've sat in restaurants in the Kingdom where women eat dinner surrounded by screens so no one but their husband can see them even though they were in a room full of other diners (to me, very bizarre). I've watched another completely covered woman in a mall in Riyadh hold an ice cream cone while her entire face was shielded by a burka, and wondered how the heck she was going to eat her scoop of mint chocolate chip before the deliciousness melted in her gloved hand.

To say that none of that experience colors the way I cover things like radical Islam would be naïve. And a lie.

When you look at the anchors who have legions of viewers night after night, day after day, they show their true selves every time out, taking a huge risk that the viewer will embrace them or reject them. Every show, every minute is an enormous gamble.

Boy, is that scary.

That's flying without a parachute. That means when you make a mistake or say something stupid (everyone does—get over it) you have to own it. You never lose showing people you're human, as long as the foundation is pretty damn solid and you don't make too many mistakes. But you definitely have to be cool with who you are. You're not perfect, the audience isn't perfect, no one is perfect, and perfect is really annoying anyway.

This isn't just about news people, you may be realizing. This idea, of just showing your cellulite, is in fact a lifestyle choice. I might even call it channeling your inner Amy Poehler. She very famously said there's a lot of power in looking silly and not caring.

If I want proof, I can just look at my children, who have no trouble whatsoever being their true selves, silly or serious or hungry or itchy. They are generally way too comfortable with themselves. Just witness the unabashed nudity that follows a bath or shower. "Here's me, world!" they trumpet way too close to the window that offers a wonderful view to anyone passing by on the street below. The bigger the belly, the better.

My older son, Thompson, for example, is full of passion. He's happy to tell you he's going to be an astronaut-inventor-scientist when he grows up. He loves, loves, loves his baby sister, Gemma. She rewards him handsomely with infant squeals whenever he smiles in her direction or bites his fingers, which (we promise) is just like a kiss.

But as loving as Thompson is, he's the first to tell me when I've droned on too long.

"Mom, I love you, I don't want to hurt your feelings, but could we stop talking about this right now?" he begs. "I'm bored of talking to you."

Okay then!

Or when he told me that my pants were too small because he noticed they were "smooshing" my fat above the waist of the pants, and if I just bought a bigger size, that fat roll would fit inside the pants, instead of "bulging out." Just being helpful!

Not to be outdone, Greyson studies the Bioré Pore Strips commercial on television and announces that after closer consideration, that's not a product that would work for me, because the spots that litter the surface of my cheeks and nose every morning are fluorescent red, and the evil blackheads eradicated in the triumphant Bioré commercial are, of course, black. He just sighs, concluding perhaps correctly that for his mommy's face, there is no hope.

But there's a part of me that thinks, you know what? They're good with themselves, and I'm good with me. I'm done pretending. About anything. I'm too old to lie. I mean, seriously. I could make up some ridiculous lie about why I came home from the dermatologist's office with a black eye. But that takes too much energy, and I'm tired. I have three kids! I need a nap. Desperately. Plus lying means I care way too much about what everyone thinks, and I just don't anymore. I'd rather just say, "Guess what. I tried filler, and the filler won." Case closed.

Now I want to be very certain to warn you: if you are going to let it all hang out and show the world the real you, you have to be completely comfortable with your red splotches and cellulite. Or put on makeup and a robe before your kids come in and smack you awake to fix breakfast. (I love the not so gentle pat-pat-pat-pat on my red-splotched cheek followed by "Mom, I'm so hungry. Sorry.")

Deciding you don't give two dimes what other people think is a tall order for anyone. Being real is the reason I put the story of my life on paper, in *Diary of a Stage Mother's Daughter*. To be sure, dredging up and parsing every childhood trauma and insecurity on paper for anyone who might be interested to read (and judge), was like voluntarily running head first into a hornet's nest. There were many times I wondered, "What the hell am I doing? Who in their right mind would not only relive their entire past but endure the personal retrospective on paper and in public? What a moron I was to agree to this!"

Some people knew the *Little House on the Prairie* me. And that me was way, way in the past. Some people knew the financial news me. I didn't need to fill in the gaps for anyone on the time in between. Life isn't one big high school reunion. And I certainly wasn't trying to capitalize on long-gone, minor Hollywood fame. I'd already rebuilt my life and my career in a new image, and books aren't terribly profitable (unless you're Hillary Clinton).

More than one friend asked me why. But not my college roommate, Debbie. I was making calls to my friends who were going to be in the book to give them fair warning of their impending public debut.

To Debbie I mused, "I'm sure you think I'm crazy, and I will save you the question. I have no idea why I'm doing this. I must be truly crazy."

She said, "Oh no, not at all. I know exactly why you're doing it. To own it. Own your story. And then put it out there. Let people say and think what they want, but you're on the record, on your terms. And then you're done. You can move on and leave it behind."

As usual, she was dead on. I didn't want to make excuses for my life, pretend what I'd been through— with my mother, the death of my sister, the love of my father, my sometimes tortured, sometimes riotously funny, very occasionally dull, and more often odd his-tory—was anything more or less than what it actually was. I wanted to lay it out, own it, and leave it where it was. I laid out the facts exactly as I remembered them, adding the caveat that everyone's childhood and ado-lescent memory is just that—their memory—and not a historical record captured on film for accuracy's sake. But I just decided to lay bare the details as I remem-ber them, without labels on anyone's behavior, and let you, the reader, be the judge.

I've never been one to throw up my hands and say, "Poor me!" I hate sympathy. Hate it. I've always felt pity is for the weak. (Oh dammit, there's another glaring flaw. Wow, they are really piling up.) I don't love for others to see me as weak and vulnerable and less than, and if you feel sorry for me, well, that's what's going on. I'm too proud to be a victim. So I certainly didn't write the book and tell the story to garner sympathy, the last thing I want. I also wasn't trying to even any score. I know I've got no bitch coming. I feel so grateful for every bit of my life. (Except the love handles I didn't realize I had until Thompson suggested bigger pants.)

But years back, I was anchoring a show on MSNBC with a woman whose warm smile shines so brightly her kids don't need a flashlight on Halloween. Contessa Brewer is so beamingly positive I've checked her purse for drugs. She became a treasured friend the moment we sat down at the same anchor desk (that's when I looked in her purse—there's nothing good in there). I trusted her, as did her audience, and she is still someone who is bravely honest at every turn. She is perfectly comfortable in her own skin.

We were hosting a show called *It's the Economy*, leaving out the word "stupid," a phrase made popular in one of the Bush elections, when once again years later the pubic could no longer ignore the obvious pain of a sluggish economy. This was right after the financial crisis, when once again politicians were forced to take their cue from the economy and markets.

We were coming off the air one day, and Contessa said, "Someone who says she's your mother is tweeting odd things at me . . . and to my mom too." She was proceeding with Contessa-like kindness and caution (think: your favorite second-grade teacher), but her tone told me she thought this was serious. Twitter was relatively new, so the full blast of Twitter trolling and trashing hadn't hit maximum volume yet. Twitter was still more of a semi-polite conversation.

I hadn't had any contact with my mother for years. Not since my sister was hospitalized near the end of her life, and my mother chose that moment to clean out the family's finances and sprint off. I was living in San Francisco with Wray at the time, and when she reached out to me, I let her know that was not cool, to say the least. And that if she wanted to continue to have a relationship with me, she needed to also be a mother to my sister, in spite of their years of struggles, and do something a bit more equitable in terms of dividing up assets with my dad. She'd chosen to go off into the wilderness on her own, and I'd shut the door on the relationship when my sister died, motherless. That's a quick synopsis, but clearly there were many tears and much pain.

Years had passed, and I hadn't heard a squeak from her, which was more than fine with me. I was an adult, and at some point you realize you can't pick your parents. You just do what you can and keep going.

But now that I was on national television again, surprise: my mother came knocking. I didn't wish to dredge all that history up for Contessa. She didn't know the story. In fact, she didn't know half the story. I didn't think the whole ugly mess needed any more discussing—with her or anyone, really. If I were completely honest, the fact that I was related to someone who would do those things shamed me all the way to my sneakers.

Contessa continued, "This person is saying weird stuff. She's calling you horrible names. A monster. Typical psycho viewer, I guess," she said, brushing off the notion that my own mother might call me such things. In a public forum. "But she's got a lot of details, something about when you did a Jell-O commercial with Bill Cosby as a child? Anyway, that's not important. I just wanted you to know there's this person saying this stuff because she's tweeting at me and my mom, so she must be tweeting at a bunch of other people you know too."

I was mortified. Here was someone I considered a good friend, and she knew nothing about my past. That's the way I was living, with all my baggage crammed into a closet and the door locked up tight. How long could that door hold out against the weight of all those bags?

In a panic, I said a truth that didn't reveal anything: "That person sounds crazy. Yikes, I would just ignore her. And tell your mom to do the same. Just ignore her."

Because when you ignore problems, they just go away, right? Isn't that how that clever bit of conventional wisdom goes? Just ignore little tiny problems, and they fix themselves and go away on their own.

Oh no, wait.

That's not it.

No, no . . . they fester and turn into giant disgusting boils or toxic cancers that kill you. That's what happens when you try to ignore little problems.

I dodged the real truth with Contessa that day. I didn't lie, but I didn't tell the truth either. Just look at the words. Still, that lie-by-omission, technical-truth-only was a wake-up call. Because I knew that if Contessa knew what I'd never told anyone who wasn't there when the family I grew up with blew up into bits, she'd be hurt that I didn't trust her enough, trust our friendship enough, to be real with her. To be authentic, to be myself.

I knew she wouldn't really think less of me for my questionable genetic heritage, or for the choices I'd made in the past about how to deal with the fallout from the family and situation into which I was born. Sure, there were hideous flaws in all those details and plenty to make someone recoil in horror. But that's not what would hurt our friendship. Or her feelings. The fact that I didn't trust her enough to let her in would.

Fast forward two years. I had written *Diary* and gave Contessa an early copy of what I'd written, before I showed the whole shebang to the publisher. She was floored. I know she was hurt that I'd kept so much a secret. But she understood, I think.

Here's the lesson I learned: Don't be tempted to pretend to be something you're not. Everyone has flaws. Be your authentic self. Let your cellulite show. Like most imperfections, it's probably not as unsightly as you think, and we're all human anyway. But when you pretend to be something you're not, or tuck away parts of you, you fail to connect with the people around you. Friends, family, partners. You cheat yourself out of an authentic life.

So many of my friends who read my first book said, "Wow, I had no idea all those things were going on with you. I wish you'd told me so I could have been there for you and eased your pain." I cheated myself out of love and support I could have used. I won't do it again.

Friends, audiences, all people, they all want the same thing. The real you. Free yourself of the burden, drop your baggage, and leave the BS at the door.

CHAPTER EIGHT

ARE YOU THERE GOD? IT'S ME, MELISSA

Warning: This is the religious chapter I told you was coming. If religion makes you squeamish, feel free to skip ahead. You won't hurt my feelings.

Little House had dominated Monday night on NBC for eight long years. Nobody owns America for that long, and viewers were increasingly ready to hitch up their wagons and look for greener, more entertaining pastures. For the very last two episodes that featured the original cast, Michael planned a doozy—a two-parter, which of course meant a cliff-hanger—that centered on the near-death experience of the Ingalls' adopted son, my older brother, James, played of course by Jason Bateman.

I went back to rewatch the episode because I was certain my memory of the events in that installment could not possibly be accurate. I was wrong.

In the story, shiny-haired James is shot by an almost comically rough posse of bank robbers in the neighboring town of Sleepy Eye. He'd gone with Pa and Isaiah and older brother Albert in order to open his first bank account (there's Michael preaching about saving money again). He found himself in exactly the wrong place at exactly the wrong time. In formulaic television fashion, violence and drama quickly ensued.

Instead of dying, James falls into one of those prime-time television comas that stretches into the following week's episode. Days go by, and James doesn't so much as blink, as friends and family slowly come to accept that he will not recover.

As my final moment on the show, paying homage to my signature move, I get one more chance to showcase the tears, storming from the dinner table and running outside to the pasture to sob on the corral railing, in the private company of a few million viewers.

And with that, we all write off James. What a great exit.

The only holdout is Pa, who refuses to believe that James will die—and this becomes the central theme of what now stands as the show's swansong story: hold onto faith, even in your darkest hour, when all evidence seems to point to the idea that your faith is, at the very least, a bit misguided.

When those around Pa tell him to let go of James because the only thing that can save the boy is a miracle, he takes this as a helpful suggestion, putting "summon a miracle" at the top of his to-do list. He says, "I've spent my whole life believing in God's word. Why shouldn't I ask for a miracle?"

Absolutely reasonable. But when the minister tries to tell Pa there is no hope, Pa responds, "God will show me the way."

Pa is on his own—an outcast, in every sense—so he builds a kind of wheelchair cart for James and lumbers off into the woods with his comatosed son. What a fantastic plan! Wait, scratch that—the plan is horrible. Not to mention bizarre.

A massive amount of time passes. How do we know? Pa turns into Grizzly Adams with a crazy-ass beard. He then decides to build an altar to God, reaching twenty feet and more to the sky, and when he is finished, he turns to James and says, "He'll come to us now. I know he will."

Right on cue, Pa is visited by an anonymous old man who appears in the forest as if from nowhere, only to disappear just as swiftly. I don't know if the man is meant to be a vision, an angel, or God himself. Whoever he is, he stays long enough to give James some soup and to admire Pa's altar.

That night, during the worst of the storm, Pa approaches the altar carrying James in his arms. Lightning strikes the cross at the top of the altar, and the surrounding terrain is lit by a force field of electricity and wonder.

Subtle.

Sure enough, James is brought magically back to life.

The most striking part of this evangelical episode isn't what's going on with the characters. Remember, this is Michael's last episode of the show. His good-bye to the original cast. He wrote the script, he directed the episode, he had his fingerprints on every scene, and I have to think that in some way this was his letter to the viewers as he left the show—to go on, by the way, to create and star in another God-themed family drama, *Highway to Heaven*, where he played an angel.

His message, and he knew his audience, was the power of absolute faith. Taking that leap. He illustrated, with his pilgrimage, that the leap is the essence of belief. To accept what you cannot prove and lean into what you cannot see to be there.

Religious faith—true, abiding, absolute faith, of the kind demonstrated by Pa Ingalls in this two-part episode—runs against my own true nature. A boyfriend once told me that he couldn't stand the fact that I need to see all the evidence for myself, work out the math with my own pencil, that I won't take anyone's word for anything. In other words, I don't accept anything on faith. That's what drew me to reporting. I loved the idea of going out to see the characters in a story myself, hearing both sides firsthand, and drawing my own conclusion. I loved to look people in the eye, and through the lens of the camera, and decide for myself if they were telling the truth. To hold the evidence of their tale in the palm of my hand, sort through and turn over each fragment with my own fingers, and spy the holes. Maybe there weren't any, but I was never willing to accept someone else's pre-packaged verdict.

Recently at a Sunday service in New York City, Reverend Stephen Bauman took the idea one step further, suggesting that doubt isn't the opposite of faith. Certainty is.

That short-circuited my brain. Of course! Certainty and faith are opposite poles of the planet. Faith means not demanding concrete evidence fit for a jury of our peers. Accepting a premise when there's no way to be *certain*.

You don't need faith if you're certain. Doubt, however, is where we all live, hoping someday to retire in the wonderful town of Faith.

I must admit, the strength of my conviction has certainly ebbed and flowed over my lifetime, but I am grateful that the thread of organized religion ran through my childhood, holding together what otherwise would have felt at times like random bits of fabric scattered on the floor. My father used to take me and my sister to Mass on Sundays. My mother never came. She would say, "There probably is a God, and I'm probably going to hell because I don't believe in Him. Either way, I'm staying home. You guys have a nice time."

I don't know how much of a fighting chance she had with faith, though. Her mother was Jewish, and on that side of the family my grandmother was mourned for dead when she married my grandfather, who was Italian and German. His name, of all things, was Adolf at a time when another Adolf was gaining infamy around the globe.

As my mom waved us good-bye, smiling while she casually mentioned her eternal damnation, I suspected her reluctance to join us was motivated by something other than an aversion to Sunday services. She wanted the house to herself. Who could blame her? She'd spent all week running us back and forth to school, then auditions, then dance lessons and horseback riding. I'd need a break from the noise too.

My father, meanwhile, was raised in a deeply observant Catholic household on the south side of Chicago. He was an altar boy, went dutifully to Sunday school, and was taught to love, honor, and fear God. He used to tell us about the time he was punched in the face by a priest at school in maybe seventh grade, and what struck me as strange, even then, was that he looked back *fondly* at this time in his life. He believed the tough love and the harsh lessons about obedience, values, and dedication to an ideal helped to shape him, when he easily could have ended up with an unsavory crowd of thugs.

Indeed, faith was so important to my father that he made a special point to weave God into my sister's and my life, even without my mother's participation. We attended a Catholic church called Our Lady of Lourdes, in the San Fernando Valley. I loved that church because there was a small playground outside, and Tiffany and I would race to the swings the moment the last prayer was read. (We would scurry outside to be first in line, trampling half the congregation to get there, which wasn't particularly charitable or Christian.)

God traveled into the week with us too. I went to a parochial elementary school, and then on to Catholic school for middle school and high school—Chaminade College Prep in the San Fernando Valley. God was in the classroom. We studied the Old and New Testaments, year after year. The Bible, like all juicy literature, sucked me in. After all, the stories were a never-ending soap opera, filled with forbidden fruit, illicit sex, bloody murders, century-long vendettas, and thunderbolts striking people from out of nowhere. Game of Thrones for the ages. And most of the material is not even remotely age appropriate!

I read those stories as parables, although I recognize many accept them as historic text. To me, they were like Aesop's fables, laced with consequence and meaning. Real faith requires a leap. I know exactly when I left the ground. It was a Thursday, at 11:17 p.m.

I've mentioned my mother's father, Adolf. We called him Grandpa Genaro, and he was probably my favorite grandparent. I know you aren't supposed to say things like that, much less feel them, but he always rolled up his pant legs and waded right into our childish exuberance. He'd show up at our house with his pockets full of stale gum, bits of candy, and coins, and he'd let my sister and me shake him down for every last Dum Dum and dime.

Pockets emptied, he'd join us in the cul-de-sac in front of our house and run next to our bikes in endless, wide, wobbly circles until we could speed off on our own.

He'd set up bases, pitch a big rubber kickball over home plate, and then chase us down, coming just short of tagging us before we scored. I can still hear the scrape of his black-laced dress shoes on the asphalt as he ran.

My mother always told me she didn't recognize this man. He wasn't the father she'd known as a small girl. She said he was pretending with me. I didn't care; I didn't believe her, either. I loved him the most. That's why when he got stomach cancer and lay dying in the hospital, I didn't think he would die. He couldn't.

For the weeks or months he was in the hospital, we'd head from school to Hollywood for an audition, then over to the downtown hospital to check in on Grandpa. This became our routine. One night we were stuck at the hospital particularly late, and my mother deposited my sister and me in a nearby waiting room. The brown pleather couches complained each time we shifted uncomfortably, the gummy fabric sticking to our skin.

I was about ten years old at the time. Tiffany and I had been asleep for a few hours. Then suddenly, my heart began racing. I was shocked by a sudden, electric jolt as my eyes flew open. Then the adrenaline melted to grief in one calm instant, and I knew he was gone.

He'd woken me up to say good-bye.

I shook my sister awake and wept. "Grandpa just died."

She was annoyed with me, as usual.

"Shut up and go back to sleep," she said. "Mom said he's not dying. Why do you always have to be so dramatic? Stop crying. Don't wake me up again."

I looked at the clock, which read 11:17 p.m. We would learn the next day that this was in fact the exact moment he died.

That event, I guess, isn't much in the way of cold, hard evidence. And if you wanted, you could certainly explain away the bolt of lightning in a million different ways. But to me, that wake-up call was just that.

As a teenager, I would pray very specifically for "the strength to find peace" in my life. That seems like an odd wish for a sixteen-year-old, and yet those exact words were my own private prayer. Joy and happiness were too big of an ask. I just wanted to sleep soundly at night, to rid the pit of my stomach of the uncertainty that haunted me.

Years later, when I lost my sister, I railed against God and wondered if I'd fallen victim to cognitive dissonance. Was I just telling myself a story, manu-facturing evidence, to make the most upsetting and unsettling parts of life make sense? Was I placating myself, tricking myself? Trying to remedy the fact that life isn't perfect, no matter how I try to control it?

Miraculously, after decades of searching, faith and family have finally led me to that peace I prayed for as a teenager, where I can quiet my mind and let go. As I look at my life today, I can't believe it. I'm surrounded by three beautiful, healthy children whom I love until my chest hurts. My husband is the thoughtful, joyful partner I didn't know could exist. He is yoga-calm but somehow makes every day a goose-bump-inducing cel-ebration of what's possible. I've never known anyone who could create those two states simultaneously. He is clever, a strong protector (what my dad would call "a real man"), and a mischievous little boy, all at once.

I get up each weekday and pack my kids into a car buzzing with chatter. They run so fast into school, Thompson usually forgets to close the car door behind him—he's so eager to see his friends.

Then I continue on another few blocks and walk through the doors of Fox News, surfing the same wave of crisp enthusiasm that swept the boys out of my car ten minutes earlier.

Every Sunday, I go with my family to church, and as I sit in the pew I'm overwhelmed with gratitude.

I cannot count my blessings, because they are too many in number. When I think about them, I am deeply humbled. I wonder why I have been chosen to be so blessed, and I worry that I'm not deserving. I take no credit for what we have. I assign no blame for the inevitable hardships that crop up in life. I know that I am deeply flawed, a controlling person, bent on trying to make everything perfect all the time.

I'm ashamed of my petty ambitions, when I've been envious of an opportunity another talented person at my office has picked up instead of me. I'm embarrassed by that base emotion and vow to do better. I know I'm meant to share what I've been given, to remember to always be thankful, and to look honestly at my failings and try to do better, every day. And my eyes fill with tears when I think of my family's love.

How did I get here?

Why am I so lucky?

I cannot answer. I can only give thanks and be humbled by the greatness of God's gifts. My life in many ways is as unbelievable and far-fetched as that final episode of *Little House* in which Charles summons a miracle.

＊━◎ ◎━＊

Decades later, we would never see an episode like James's resurrection on broadcast television, right smack dab in the middle of prime time. So much of mainstream society has become secular. Most people don't feel comfortable weaving God into everyday conversation at all. My mother-in-law always says, "Religion and politics are not polite dinner conversation. Avoid them!" Her point is the topics are too personal, too heated, too divisive for banter. You end up highlighting your differences and making people around you feel judged or awkward. She's a real estate broker, and the last thing sales people of any type want to do is make people uncomfortable in their presence.

In most workplaces most of us wouldn't mention religion at all, ever. When I worked in the news department for CNBC and NBC, God was never mentioned. To say anything religious was to risk offending someone in the audience—or worse, to jeopardize your credibility as a reporter.

But even in a culture that tries to push God to the side, we need guiding principles. We need a context within which to teach our kids to do the right thing even when they think no one is looking. We need a common framework. A reason to be consistently decent. Try telling your kids why they shouldn't just take a wallet found in the back of a cab. Why they shouldn't cut in line when everyone's back is turned. Without the basic tenets of religion—in Christianity, for example, Jesus telling us to care for and treat the people around us with at least as much generosity and compassion as we would want for ourselves—*why* is harder than you might imagine.

I realized when I had kids, putting into words the moral responsibility we have to everyone and everything around us is precisely why our current culture ended up worshipping the environment. See, if you recognize the planet as God's creation, you can imagine why you shouldn't litter, or waste water, or snuff out whole species of animals. But if there's no God, then there's no one watching when you throw a hamburger wrapper out the window of your moving car. That's a problem. So someone started the notion of going green, and stretched the idea into a mini religion. And along the way, the miracle of multiplying loaves of bread has morphed into recycling.

We need a framework in order to divide the things around us into piles of good and evil, right and wrong. You either share what you have because that's the model Jesus lived and taught, or you can hand over what you've earned to be redistributed in the name of Socialism. Without God, in my view, the liberal, left-wing progressive political agenda has taken the place of religion. Churches and close-knit communities used to be the centers of charity, the safety net for those down on their luck, but now all that has been replaced by the government. The problem is that I for one find Uncle Sam an unsatisfying preacher. His lay leaders in Washington don't seem to have the purest intentions.

The framework to avoid that end, though, can come in the form of any religion. I wouldn't dream of implying that Christianity had the market cornered on coming up with reasons to convince you to be a good person—far from it. Almost everyone at my Catholic high school was Catholic, of course. But when I got to Harvard, many of the friends I made were devoutly Jewish and tried to do the right thing in the name of Faith.

My roommate Debbie and I seemed to be polar opposites from the outset. She walked into our dorm that first year ripe from the Freshman Outdoor Project (by ripe, I mean smelly). She'd responded to a flier I'd received over the summer and wisely assumed was a prank. Students were invited to FOP to meet and bond while camping in the wild, digging holes in which to defecate, and then bury what they'd done. I hadn't pictured getting to know my future classmates with a small shovel in my hand.

When Debbie crossed the threshold of the room we'd share for the next year, the scent of too many days spent outdoors (without running water) trailed her. Amazingly, though, she left behind any preconceived notions she might have about me, her utterly other new roomie. Contrary to what almost anyone might have expected, she seemed to just accept my bleached blonde hair, my painted nails and eyelids, and the avalanche of clothes that tumbled out of the closet (which apparently was somehow supposed to also be hers.) You might have thought we'd blend about as well as garlic and vanilla incense. Instead Debbie opened both our minds and let in some fresh air.

Debbie challenged my way of thinking at every turn but supported me wholeheartedly when I joined my only right-leaning friend on campus, Matt, at a table in the student union trying to drum up members for the Harvard Republican Club. I've always considered myself an independent—if anything, maybe a libertarian—but I thought I'd give this a shot. Talk about looking like we were peddling a prank! Imagine two freshmen parked behind a folding table trying to get other students at a liberal arts university to self-identify as Republicans. We were a very, very exclusive club, almost to the point of being a secret society. Either that or a totally shunned and ignored gathering of outcasts that other students spit on, depending on how you looked at it.

Over the next four years, Debbie taught me that although we were total opposites, we were in fact, pretty much the same, once you peeled back the surface and examined our values, for example. Religion was another item on the different/same list. We may have belonged to different denominations, but underneath, our core values—to love God, to show compassion to those around us, to be open to the ideas and opinions of those around us, to strive to be better, kinder, more generous people at all times—those were the same.

But we don't always see our commonality hidden beneath our differences, especially when the subject is religion. Around this time, I was walking on campus with Matt and our other friend, Michelle, who had received a letter from her rabbi back home. He'd written: "Now that you are of age, it's important for you to remember to date Jewishly." We all roared at the adverb. What could he have possibly meant? I can't do any jokes here, because I'm not Jewish, but I will let you imagine the quips that came from Matt and Michelle. We laughed so hard we almost had to borrow Debbie's shovel. But we knew what he meant. Don't stray from the herd, lady.

Unlike Michelle's rabbi, I didn't think I cared what religion my husband was. In fact, when Wray and I started dating, I don't remember even talking about the subject much at all. We were young, in our early twenties, staying out late on Saturday nights, so the best we could do on Sunday was brunch. At 2:00 p.m. We'd worship grilled cheese with bacon and a slice of tomato at EJ's down the block.

But when we got engaged, Wray suggested his minister from growing up perform the ceremony. I was a little surprised he felt that connection, given that the minister would have to travel all the way from Florida to California to do the deed. Until then, I'd just assumed we'd raise our kids Catholic.

He suggested we try each other's religion on for size, but like any good negotiator, Wray did his best to stack the deck before I'd even sat down to play cards. First he went with me to a Catholic service on the Upper West Side, for the slightly boring but heavenly calming church experience that I'd come to accept as the norm. Wray said he didn't get that much from the priest's message. What did he expect? Sit for an hour, sing a few songs, think about trying to be a decent person the following week, and ask forgiveness for blaring the horn at the garbage truck that blocked the street for nine solid minutes. Critical and analytical thinking that cracked open the world to shed new light on its core was setting his sights a bit too high.

Then Wray took me to a Methodist Church across town. Unbeknownst to me, the minister was the type of speaker you'd hire to bring a graduating audience of thousands to their feet. The sanctuary ceiling reached to heaven, displaying God's majesty with thousands of jeweled tiles in a sparkling navy, flecked with bits of amber and slate that glinted and glimmered like the furthest stars in an endless night sky. The sermon was the first I'd ever heard that plunged the power of faith headfirst into everyday life. Unlike a priest who lived cloistered among his kind, this minister was a regular, run-of-the-mill married guy with kids, subject to the same tests of patience as the rest of us: unpredictable teenage children, a wife who probably gets furious when he uses the last of the soap without replacing it, and a cable man who never fails to not show up. He had the exact same frame of reference in which to couch God's message, making his sermons hysterical and heartbreaking in equal measure.

Wray totally hosed me.

Now, years later, we attend these services with our children, who head upstairs to Sunday school for the same lesson the adults are receiving in the sanctuary below. The kids' service is chopped up into child-sized portions, aided by guitar-driven songs that can involve silly hand motions, and coloring books that let the kids fill in God's message in any shade they see fit.

On the way home, we always take a beat to share and compare what we each thought we heard. "So what did you guys talk about?" Wray opens each time.

"We talked about what if I was really, really good and always cleaned my room and always did my homework," Greyson starts, looking sideways at his brother, who sighs and rolls his eyes on cue. "But Thompson went outside and played, and messed everything up and didn't do anything he was supposed to and when he walked in the front door you decided to throw *him* a party! What if that happened! Would that be fair?"

"Sure would!" Thompson grins gleefully.

I have to hand it to the Methodists. The format is a very clever way to get the whole family on the same page.

On Monday when I head into the office, I usually throw the program from the service into my bag. When I unpack my water bottle and fish around for the bills I need to pay, I see the cream-colored pamphlet, a physical prompt not to strangle any of my coworkers that day. I know myself well enough to own that I need a daily reminder of my intention to be decent, as deep into the week as possible.

⊷⊫⊜ ⊙⊒⊰⊶

If you spend any time quietly contemplating life in a pew, you can't help but do a deep dive into your own faults. In the end, I know my biggest flaw happens to also be something that much of the world rewards in spades. As I've mentioned, I'm a controlling person, bent on perfection. You could eat off the floor of my apartment. I mean it. Stop by for a meal. And I love to purge closets with abandon. Throwing things out is one of my greatest delights in life. No item is safe, no matter how precious. If threads come loose, a wheel pops off, or the motor dares to hum at the wrong time, you can kiss it good-bye. When my kids can't find a lightsaber or a Pokémon card, they sigh and say, "Oh no, Mom threw that down the garbage chute." They don't even bother to whimper, things go missing so often. Come sit on my couch, and you'll be surrounded by pillows that have been beaten and plumped within an inch of their lives. And I completely freak out if my kids leave their toys in the living room rather than dragging them back to the playroom where they belong.

And yes, I do realize this qualifies as a disorder.

I am a nightmare to live with, but this sickness has also propelled me to success in school and at work. Teachers and bosses love discipline. (Though I've not tried to get hired in any of the relaxation fields, like leading meditation.) To the naked eye, I have a Protestant work ethic. To my family, I'm in need of therapy, preferably on an in-patient basis.

I try to take a breath and stop myself from driving everyone around me to the nearest bar. And that breath is often faith. I know any success is really God's and not mine. I can't take full credit for my achievements. By the same token, every imperfection is not my fault. There's the things I must try every day to do better, like being kind instead of cutting, and the things I must let go and simply embrace, like my scream-inducing feet. They are a podiatrist's dream, riddled with everything that could be both wrong and revolting. And they are totally beyond my control. A permanent reminder to accept what I cannot change. Like the fact that I'm aging.

But here's the payoff to that reluctant acceptance: by living an honest life, bunions and cellulite plainly visible to the world, I am free. This is me, take it or leave it. Not the guarded me or the perfect me. The real me.

The lesson: faith led me to honesty and ultimately to acceptance; that acceptance led to the peace and freedom I'd always longed for.

And, like Charles Ingalls, I've learned to allow myself to believe in miracles.

When I was looking for pictures to include in this book, to visually evoke the memory of what for me was long ago, I told my editor Amanda in frustration that I didn't have much. That's another price of the break I made from my mother: I don't have many childhood photos.

"We used everything I have in the first book. I have no other pictures," I said in frustration before hanging up the phone and leaving my office to get more coffee. When I returned, a mysterious yellow envelope had appeared on my desk, which I quickly sliced open with no regard to what was inside. A few dozen square, fuzzy photos fell out, showing me and various actors and stage hands behind the scenes of *Little House on the Prairie*, posing in front of the prop truck or fooling around the set between takes.

I shivered.

Each one showed an image I'd laid eyes on before but hadn't seen in so long that I'd assumed it was just an invention of my imagination, a snapshot of a real memory that didn't actually exist on film.

The letter with the photos read:

"Enclosed are some pictures I hope you will enjoy. They were sent to my mother by your grandmother. She and my mom were friends for over 40 years . . ."

I gently opened the yellowed handwritten page that held the photographs and looked at my grandmother's unmistakably elegant handwriting, bragging to her old friend back home that she'd just returned from set-sitting me on *Little House*, and here were some photos to prove it.

All this sent to me by a total stranger, Barbara Mullert, who had been cleaning up some of her now hundred-year-old mother's papers when she came across these photos that she thought I might like to have back.

How could they have crossed my desk, thirty-five years later, at the exact second I desperately needed precisely these photos? You could call this uncanny coincidence incredibly good fortune. To me, that's just too much of a stretch. At that moment, as I tried not to let my tears spill onto the delicate photos and ruin them, I couldn't help but feel some force put those in my hands at that moment. A favor? A message from another grandparent? I'll call this event my own small miracle.

I do have faith.

CHAPTER NINE

TURN IT OFF; THEN TURN
IT BACK ON AGAIN

I n the first five years after college, I moved seven times. That's a lot of tape and boxes. Even still, I had nothing on the Ingalls family, which, if you read the books, had everything from malaria to locusts to near starvation to broken promises from the government (yes, even then) chase them from one home to the next, all their hard work down the drain, only to forge deeper into enemy territory and back again, hoping for a better outcome. Unlike me, this group had to deconstruct and rebuild their furniture, not to mention their actual house in many cases, to get a move on. They really did "pull up stakes." Saving the nails from your now-destroyed dream house so that you can rebuild and restart seems like insult to injury to me. But they got out their few tools and began collecting.

What choice did they have? They could have just lain down on the road and waited for the next passing wagon to put them out of their misery. But the roads were thinly traveled. That might have taken awhile.

Instead they pressed on with feigned confidence. These scrappy folks personified one of the most essential lessons of survival in any century: the art of reinvention.

When Michael was pretending to do this in front of the camera, he was living that burden in real life as well. When *Bonanza* ended, he dreamed up the *Little House* show. He had no idea if the story that delighted mostly little girls on paper would translate to America's living rooms. I bet the original script looked as bizarre to the network chiefs who gave the project the green light as the scenes had looked to me before my original audition. But they took a flier on him, and he rewarded them with a mint of cash from advertisers who couldn't wait to sell dish soap to the millions of people who tuned in every week to see if this would be the time the elements got the best of Charles.

When I came on *Little House*, my job was to reinject some little-kid energy into the show. The original cast had grown long in the tooth, and frankly so had the concept. Giving a facelift to the aging hit didn't do the trick, and Michael did what all guys with everything on the line do when faced with defeat. He blew up the show. And I mean that literally: he strapped dynamite to the old set in the Simi Valley and watched the last ten years of his life combust in a fiery thunder cloud that eclipsed the sun. The *New York Times* called the show's huge send-off "perhaps the most apocalyptic valedictory to any television series in history."

Amazingly, when the dust settled, he washed, rinsed, and repeated the essence of the *Bonanza/Little House* concept one more time, with *Highway to Heaven*. The same formula, repackaged, and no less successful.

Each time he hit reset, or lit the fuse on the powder keg, Michael had to get everyone on the project to believe that he could recast the same magic in a new form. But I always wondered if he was 100 percent confident that when he turned his hit machine back on, a new winner would appear. He could have taken his millions and retired to his stunningly serene mansion in Malibu. But then he would no longer be the King of Reinvention.

When I was in college, I worked for a technical support team at Harvard Business School. That job is still one of the best ones I've ever had. A handful of undergrads (all women, shockingly enough) helped the students who had returned from the corporate world for more management training (95 percent of them men) do their casework on a network of computers in the rooms of their relatively lush and well-appointed B-school dorm.

Simple enough. We all used some type of Apple desktop device to write our papers in the undergraduate dorms. How tough could this job be? I can tell you, helping with computers beat the hell out of chopping vegetables in the basement the way I'd done the previous spring.

As tech support team members, we would sit by a phone at a desk in the lobby, drink the free soda that was on tap for these spoiled B-school brats, and wait for one of them to call and say they couldn't find the button to power up their machine. Or figure out how to reload the paper. In the meantime, I could sit in luxury, do my homework, and fill up on soda and snacks.

"Cushy" didn't even capture this gig. It rocked. If more people knew about this job, they would have been beating down the door to steal my spot, so I tried to keep it hush-hush.

Right at this precise moment in time, the Internet became a thing. I remember the head of the Program in Management Development explaining to me that I was to use a telephone cord to plug the Macs they had placed in all the rooms into the phone jack, and that way, all the computers could chitchat with each other, and people on the computers could chitchat with each other too using a concept called email.

"So, this electronic letter business . . . " I began, rolling my eyes at the very idiocy.

"Email. It's called 'email,'" the senior coordinator corrected with his superior, South African accent.

"Right. Whatever. People are going to sit in their bleak little dorm rooms and type out long letters to their friends. Who will then read them, reflect on their nuanced thoughts and clever retorts, and then . . . rather than say, get a beer, or watch television, or hang themselves, write a long letter in return? Like hermits. Alone. Typing. To friends. Quietly in their sad little rooms. Rather than just simply picking up the phone and talking? Like, say, human beings would, for example. That's the idea? That's the basic premise? That's the stupidest thing I've ever heard. Hello? We have telephones. Everyone would prefer to actually talk," I said, making my hand into a little phone and speaking into my fingers, just in case he was too much of a dork himself to understand the mechanics of telephonic devices.

"Indeed," he replied, clearly nonplussed that I seemed to have forgotten who was in charge of hiring and firing on the tech support team.

"And what are these hermits paying by the minute? Is it cheaper than long distance rates? I have AT&T long distance, and I can call like crazy after ten . . ."

"It's free, actually," he grinned, very pleased with himself.

"Oh yes. That is a genius business plan! It's free. Democrats must have dreamed up this idea. What a great business model. Give a bad product away for free! Are we still at Harvard Business School?" I roared at what an obvious loser this idea was.

I did not invest in AOL.

Luckily for my employment needs at the time, the students were even less technically savvy than I. They were part of a specific, small program that sent middle

managers to summer camp for a semester to bone up
and retrain (not in technology, obviously). They were
a bit older than the normal business school students
and were used·to having abundant luxuries like assis-
tants and expense accounts.

They expected to fly first class at all times. I ex-
celled at this job because I realized I was more Don
Draper's lovely 1950s flight attendant and less a
grumpy car mechanic.

When students would call my outpost in the
lobby and explain (whine about) their problem, I'd log
onto their desktop remotely (which was super creepy
and demonstrated to me early on in the tech revolu-
tion that people could cyber enter your dorm room/
bedroom and watch your screen without your knowledge). Or I'd walk up to their room and fix whatever
technical problem they were having while doing their
homework. (Oh goodness, Brooks, you have to plug in
the machine for the electricity from the wall to reach
the nice cube on the desk and light up the screen!)

All that . . . for $20 an hour. $25 once I worked
my way up to manager. Woot! Woot!

Of course a trip up to their room could be dicey,
presenting some fairly obvious hazards. A bit like de-
livering room service when the occupant might answer
in his robe. (Ideally closed, but there's no guarantee.)
Plus these (mostly) men were at adult summer camp,
taking a break from their normal jobs (spouses). And
they were pretty used to perks.

I learned rather rapidly to move quickly and deliberately, and very graciously ease my way out of any inappropriate offers or suggestions about what we could do when the offending computer was remedied, while leaving all doors propped open at all times. My goal was to help those who might be afflicted with a mild case of midlife crisis not to make a lunge that would prove embarrassing in the morning. I was Grace Kelly helping with homework and guiding on manners.

I also had to inspire their confidence by making their computer work. And this is how I learned the *Greatest Secret Known to Tech Support Professionals and NASA Rocket Scientists Everywhere*.

The holy grail of tech training, at the heart of every manual, every course, every secret launch code:

When it stops working, shut it off, and then turn it back on again.

Hit restart.

That's it! That's the complete bucket of bolts. The whole enchilada. The entire guidebook. The graduate, summa cum laude thesis. Don't tell anyone I told you. But that's all the magic there is. In tech support, and in life too.

Restart. Reboot. Recast. Reinvent. Call it what you like.

Also, replace the toner. That's good too. But mostly, just turn it off. Then back on again.

As I told you at the top, Michael Landon was the master at rebooting. He reinvented himself when *Little House* got old, and the cast got old, but how do you apply that to the problem of aging itself? Blow up your face?

I'm not going to lie, aging is a bitch. They say it's better than the alternative, but how do we really know that? Look on the bright side . . . wait, no. Don't do that. The light on the Bright Side is very unflattering. Just awful. In fact, turn out the lights at every possible opportunity.

Okay, so putting a little positive spin on the whole aging thing, I care less about how wide my bottom is now that I am officially aging, and I guess that's a plus. I'm recasting my priorities. My friend Mary says, "You realize at a certain age, it's your ass or your face."

You know what? She's right. If you starve your ass back down to just double the size it was in college, your face then looks roughly three hundred years old. So what's the point? Are you going to walk into your high school reunion ass first? I don't recommend that. You will fall right on those buttocks you've starved to perfect. That's no good.

Plus, I have a hard time seeing my rear in the mirror these days. I have to contort and twist, and for what? To burn into my brain for all of eternity the disturbing image that every single person who has ever walked behind me sees but is too afraid (horrified) to mention? That (without Spanx) I look like I'm hiding two mail sacks in my britches? I know if I see myself from this angle, I will never wear white pants or a bathing suit or leave the house or strip down to take a shower again. So why bother worrying about the rear view?

Meanwhile, the thousands of tiny wrinkles that multiply overnight like evil, possessed rabbits are right there staring me in the face when I'm least prepared, first thing in the morning! I'm going with face over ass, I've firmly decided. Obviously much of that decision is based on bacon. So what. Sue me.

After my BLT, I have a couple of good, go-to tricks to stall (a bit) the horrifying slide toward *older.* First, surround yourself with people who are slightly younger, and then completely forget there's any age difference between you and them. Not like ten years younger—that has the reverse effect and (sadly) serves to reinforce your heinous agedness. Terrible! Instead, employ someone like four years younger. My sister-in-law, Ali, is ideal for this purpose. In my mind, we were born on the same day. In fact, when someone (like an ER doctor) asks how old I am, I give them Ali's birthday without skipping a beat. I guess this would be problematic if I were being quizzed by border security, but I'll cross that bridge (border) when I get to it.

Reinventing myself as Ali seemed like the perfect way to hit reset on the aging process, until I bucked up against Wray's two much younger cousins. Madelyn and Caroline are about fifteen years younger than we are. (I'm really guessing and rounding with that

estimate because I would sooner duct-tape hot coals
to my armpits than actually ask them what year they
were born and do the math.) Anyway, they are super
young, which used to be a huge boost. How great to
introduce two much younger girls as cousins. Jackpot,
you say. Indeed! If a jackpot is a smelly, wet stink-
bomb that blows up in your face and covers you with
old age, then, yes, jackpot!

I'll tell you why: Madelyn's birthday party. Madelyn's birthday party should have been great (and
very youngifying). The celebration of youth was at a
very hip bar in the West Village. I arrived fashionably
late. And let me be honest, I looked *phenomenal*. Tight
black dress, hair cooperating on a relative basis, loads
of black eyeliner, enough slick lip gloss for a whole
team of tiny fairies to ice skate across my smile. Phenomenal! I was blending in seamlessly with her young
friends and had begun to think about ditching Ali as
my age-guise when the girl next to me asked:

"So . . . are you the aunt from Westchester?"

I have to explain exactly on how many levels this
was the most vicious and evil thing anyone has ever
said to me in my whole entire life. First of all, Westchester is a suburb where young people go to die and
then have children. It's quite lovely and very upscale,
but the battle to not age is pretty much lost when you
forsake the city and move out to the burbs. I mean,
the only thing that was ever young about *Sex in the
City* was the city, right? So stay in the city if battling

age is important to you (over comfort, or schools, or space, or fresh air).

And what was that word that came right before "from Westchester"? Don't tell me, because I didn't hear it, and if I did, I would have gone all reality TV smack-down on that (otherwise I'm sure very nice but obviously very nearsighted) girl.

I didn't get mad or say anything I would regret. In fact, I was very polite and simply responded, "I'm Madelyn's daughter from the Lower East Side. But if you'll excuse me, I'm going to go anywhere else and talk to someone whose eyeballs are still connected to their brain."

My husband has no problem when people think he's Madelyn and Caroline's uncle! I even caught him referring to himself as the uncle just to avoid the confused look on the other person's face that usually surfaces when he says "cousin." That's really horrifying. I slapped him very hard for this decision and blamed his dementia.

I don't know what it's like to be an aging man. But I do know that you can't teach them new tricks. You can't reinvent their habits. So I say, Why try? Here's what I mean. When we move into a new apartment, I don't try to tell my husband where to put his dirty clothes or in what cabinet his shaving cream will reside. Instead, I let him roam around his new home and litter his dirty underwear and razors wherever tossing those essentials feels natural. Think of me as an anthropologist, whispering a running commentary in a British accent, just observing nature for another gentle documentary on public television.

When I find a heap of razors next to a stick of deodorant (sans cap), I merely construct a cabinet around them and voila! That's his spot. Similarly, when enough pairs of boxers reliably accumulate in one spot, I silently tiptoe in and slide a hamper in that location. I don't trouble myself if that place is right in the middle of the living room, or next to the car in the garage. Doesn't matter if that seems like not the best spot for a hamper or a medicine cabinet. Because over this matter, we have no control. To place the receptacles elsewhere is utterly futile! This is where this particular mammal is shedding his skivvies and toiletries, and nothing can change that. Not even his mother. I know, because Wray's mother, Martha, asked me how I trained her son to be so tidy, and I explained that I did no training at all. I wouldn't dream of it! She mentioned that she nagged and harangued him his entire life to put his clothes in the hamper and pick up his room and no matter what she threatened, he would never do it. Even though she barked, and barked, and barked, and barked.

Hmmmm. You don't say? So you nagged and complained and jumped up and down with your fists in the air, and he still didn't do what you wanted? Almost like his calm, blank reaction was *intentional* as he drove you even battier? I feel there's a lesson in there somewhere.

On a completely unrelated note (which is completely related obviously,. but don't tell Martha), I would never dream of training my husband to do anything. Training men positively doesn't work. I promise. They just end up turning on their trainers like so many white tigers in Vegas and ripping them limb from limb (or wandering off with a nice quiet, low-key, younger trainer).

Don't do it. Skip the training. This has nothing to do with aging. I just didn't want to forget to warn you about one of the most essential lessons in life. I'm writing it here in case I somehow forget to tell my daughter. That person standing next to you at the altar at your wedding is the very best version of that guy, on the best behavior that he can possibly muster. If you think of him as a fixer-upper you're going to improve over time, reinvent in a better form, if you will, you are in for a very big (heartbreakingly painful) letdown. This is the thing you cannot turn off and turn back on again: your partner. You can't improve him or her just as they can't improve you. You've both been campaigning for the job of lifelong spouse, and once either of you is elected to office, you'll do nothing but relax and regress, not get neater, thinner, or nicer to the other person's family. In truth, I will tell all my children this because this hard truth has nothing to do with gender.

You can't reinvent your partner. Ask anyone who has gone to counseling hoping the therapist will take their side so they can finally reign triumphant over who was right. They didn't walk out satisfied.

What were we talking about before that? Right, the soul-crushing plight of aging. Yes! Back to that.

Okay, so what doesn't work in the quest to stay young(ish) is *lying about your age.* I know, because I had two very clever schemes that were brilliantly devised to do just that, and both ignited into flames right in front of my aging face.

The first (which I still think was divinely magnificent in its simplicity) was that every time I changed jobs or moved television markets, I would just knock one or two years off my age. I started when I was twenty-three, an age when no sane person would begin subtracting. Genius! My plan was chugging along brilliantly until the most villainous of enemies thwarted it and ruined my life.

The Internet.

God, I hate the Internet. Now I can't lie about anything ever to anyone.

They can just use the Google and instantly know I'm a lying lunatic. That just sucks. In the age of the Internet, you can't reinvent yourself using a pack of lies, but I already urged you to be authentic anyway, so you knew this idea was doomed from the get-go. (That was a test.)

The second plan was less thought out and back-fired in gloriously awful ways I could never have anticipated. It started simply enough when my six-year-old son asked me how old I was and I said with a smile, "Twenty-three." He beamed with pleasure. As did I.

I didn't realize he would keep a running tally from that day forward.

Every year, he marked off another year. So when he turned eight, and he told another family his mother was twenty-five, they looked a little stunned (this was Manhattan, where young mothers are forty-five). But then when they looked at me, they laughed.

They LAUGHED.

Okay, I deserved that. And I could laugh along with the joke (after a moment). This age shaming seemed only fair since, for the previous two years, I had been (happily) two decades younger than my husband in the eyes of my children. I won't lie here: I thought the fact that I sold them on this age difference spoke volumes about my relative appearance, and it is possible that I did a touch of gloating in and out of my husband's presence.

But God evened the score further when my sons came with us to my twentieth college reunion. They only had to read the first welcome sign before they said, "Wait a minute . . . " Their gotcha-inspired glee led them to shout my age from the nearest rooftop, at every opportunity.

Amazingly, the backfiring of this hastily hatched scheme worsened from there. The very next time I told them they could never, ever tell a lie, they chimed in (like smiling hyenas):

"Like the lie you told us about your age?"

Very nice.

The only good thing about aging (yes, my children, blah blah blah) . . . but really, the only good thing about growing old(ish) was that *Oprah narrated my life*. I'm not even kidding you. I swear, this really happened! The show is called *Where Are They Now?* So that's not entirely flattering, as the title implies that the subjects of the show are both old and (now somewhat) forgotten. But I brushed that off the second I heard Oprah's deep, warm tones say with a smile, "You remember this little girl?"

THE SMILING PICTURE THAT FILLED THE SCREEN WAS ME! I DID REMEMBER THAT LITTLE GIRL! SHE WAS ME! *ME!*

I screamed this in my living room, and my family looked at me as if I were stark, raving mad. And I didn't care one ounce. Because OPRAH WAS NARRATING MY LIFE!

OPRAH!

Beat that, twenty-something bitches!

Besides, Oprah doesn't care about aging. So why should I? She says she's earned every wrinkle. Though she doesn't really have any. Also she sleeps on a mattress filled with money, with pillows cased in money,

which she burns after one use and replaces with another money pillowcase sewn of bills of higher denominations. They are good for the complexion, I guess.

So Oprah looks fantastically ageless, but for the
rest of us, age is a mudslide that starts mid-forehead
and just keeps slipping and sagging until you need
bigger shoes to house what time and gravity has sent
tumbling south.

I always wondered why my mother said, "Oh her
skin is so lovely!" To me the epidermis was the larg-
est, most useless organ I had, made to get burned and
chapped and cut very finely by paper. Not to be admired or envied. I didn't appreciate my youthful skin
until typhoon season arrived and ushered in the start
of the Great Mudslide. I guess eventually I can get it
all stapled back up to my scalp. All the Upper East
Side ladies do it. But it never looks the same. Just
more stapled.

In fact, there's this frightening phenomenon men
on the Upper East Side of Manhattan describe, in
which they are walking behind a woman, with narrow,
fit hips, and thigh-high boots, and flowing, luxurious
blond hair, and they speed up to get a look at her face
and instead of happening upon a twenty-something
delight, they realize they've accidentally sidled up on
a seventy-something woman with inflated water wings
for lips.

Now, shame on those men for being horrified instead of celebrating that this woman has toned and

tamed her body and hair to resemble someone fifty years younger. But I'm betting the man's suddenly sour expression washes away that victory in a snap. What a shame.

Clearly I work in a business that makes aging especially difficult. Our society worships youth, nowhere more than on television, where viewers turn to lose themselves in the fantasy of that day's ideal. I certainly can't complain that women who work in television, like myself, feel more pressure to look young, thin, and wrinkle-free while showing as much cleavage, leg, and skin as possible in the tightest dresses we can stretch over our hips and shoulders. And for the men on television, it's all about the exact number of hair follicles still attached to their scalps. That's what we signed up for. With our eyes wide open. Moaning about the pressure to fit the (minute) mold would be like applying for a job at Hooters and then complaining about the uniforms. I raised my hand and volunteered for this. So I have no one to blame but myself (I hate that; I always prefer to blame someone else, like my husband or my mailman or a random stranger on the street).

But here's the thing I may have glossed over. When Oprah narrated my life, and asked where I was now, her producers picked me at least in part because they thought where I was now was completely different, unexpected, and perhaps inspiring. I'm sincerely humbled by that, and in the midst of my aging crisis

I realized that I managed to pull off Michael's very famous reincarnation trick. Instead of lying down in the road and dying after an entire career of acting, I totally rebooted and found something else that made my heart sing. And here's my point: I don't have to be afraid of aging, which is death in television, a business that revolves around youth. I've hit reset once; I can do it again. Instead of being afraid, I can just blow the whole thing up and bravely reinvent. Who knows? Maybe I'll become a writer.

So many people have had that same terrifying sensation: Now what? Holding on by our fingernails to what's slipping away—"what" could be love, after heartbreak or divorce. We could give up on love, on personal connection. But instead we chose to take the risk and hit restart. To let go of the past and try again.

The lesson to me can be summed up like this: when what you've known isn't working any longer, the world becomes a terrifying place. We try to hold onto careers, relationships, our youth (yikes!). But just like your old faithful PC, the best thing you can do is to be brave, turn it off, and then turn it back on again.

Who knows? What appears could be the best version yet.

SO WHAT?

When Katherine MacGregor took the set as Harriet Oleson, she bulldozed the furniture. There was nothing quiet or subtle about her performance, and that's the way she liked it.

"Take a good look at her," my mother said. "She makes the most of every second she's on camera. She's practically chewing on the scenery, but you can't take your eyes off her."

Katherine frightened me with the volume of her cackle. Before our first scene together, she took me aside to chat, her warm, fleshy hand pulling me to a set of director's chairs in the shadows.

"You're supposed to be so adorable, so irresistible, Missy, that your cuteness spirits me out of bed and right back to life!" She waved her arms wildly over her head as if someone had hit her with a cattle prod.

"So let me see you! Are you really so cute? Show me those eyes . . ." she tickled me and tucked me into her side. I couldn't help loving her.

Katherine personified so many of the lessons I've tried to share in these pages. Who could be more resilient? She dug her nails into the entire run of the show, never allowing her character to lose prominence or get written off, because she invented an essential role for herself in the drama as the *lovable villain*, industriously adding a bit of physical comedy like taking a pie in the face (which she did more than once). She loved to be the butt of the joke and didn't mind looking utterly ridiculous in the process.

She engaged with me to bring out my best performance, even though I was just a little kid. That was kind, but the gesture also enhanced *her* performance and made the scene the best it could be.

Far from being the lunatic she played on the screen, she didn't let herself get caught up in how many scenes she wasn't in. Instead she threw herself into every scene, every second the camera was trained on her.

As for the art of reinvention, she was a trained theater actress performing classics on stage like *Who's Afraid of Virginia Woolf?*, but rather than look down her nose at television the way so many did, she wisely followed the money to *Little House*, playing her lines now mostly for laughs rather than highbrow excellence.

And who could watch her on television and ever doubt that acting was her true passion?

I wrote these chapters in the spirit of Katherine, hoping to make you laugh at every time in life I've taken a pie to the face. I'm as clumsy and flawed as you, if not more so. And I don't care! Perfect is boring, and it's a lie. Besides, I've learned so much licking that delicious whipped cream off my face.

You just can't kill me. I can get back up, strap my family to my back, and soldier on. I know because I've scraped myself up off the ground before. I'm not going to lie down by the side of the road and die. And I'll press far past that place where I was knocked down.

I sincerely believe that in real life, the good guy wins in the end, even though there are long stretches when the villain is way out in the lead. Just be patient. The story won't end that way. Don't be tempted to take up that villain's mean-spirited weapons for yourself.

Find your passion, what you truly want, and don't let yourself be distracted by the fear that others are getting ahead of you or the worry you'll never succeed. You'll just drive yourself crazy and put yourself further from your goal. That's lunatic behavior. Don't be your own worst enemy!

Don't always feel pressure to lean in. Know when it's time to sit down and take a load off rather than measuring yourself against supposed superheroes around you. They're not as super as they look!

Be economic in everything you do. That doesn't mean being cheap, but making the most of every dollar and every opportunity.

Have faith, and know that there are angels like Briana and her family in this world. They are the miracles I never would have expected.

Always, always laugh at yourself.

And when all else fails, turn it off and then back on again. Reboot. The reinvention can be even better than the first version, if you take that risk. ▪

These are all the lessons I try so hard to live and to share with my children.

I was snuggled up next to my kids watching a show about outer space. As the galaxy glittered and hummed, held together by the magic of an invisible rubber band–like force, Thompson said, "Physics and the universe are so beautiful, they make me cry."

That's passion.

Find the thing that's so beautiful it makes you weep. Go get it, embrace it, ingest it, hold onto it. When it knocks you down, give yourself a second to lick your wounds, but then get up and chase it all over again. Don't drive yourself and the people around you crazy on the way. Laugh often and loudly, embracing the fact that none of us will ever be perfect. Don't waste time, money, or love. If you pass someone along the road who's fallen, help them up. God will send someone to help you when you stumble as well. It is the little miracles that make life sing.

ACKNOWLEDGMENTS

T hank you to my family for standing by me in this process, again. For all the times I said, "Mommy has to write now," and you understood. Wray, Thompson, Greyson, and Gemma, you give my life meaning. I love you all beyond your wildest imagination.

Thank you also to my Dad, Tony Francis, who has always supported me and encouraged me, no matter how high or impossible to climb the mountain ahead appears. And to all the Thorns, Garritys, and Dillaboughs who never fail to provide a boisterous and gleeful cheering section.

Thank you to Amanda Murray, who tirelessly sorted my musings for a second time. Without your wise and patient guidance, it's all just babble. Many thanks to my clever and creative publishing director, Georgina Levitt, and everyone else at Weinstein Books, and my wonderful agent, Mel Berger.

Thank you to the many friends, Fox colleagues, and family mentioned in these pages who provided inspiration and provoked thought. If I've embarrassed you, please accept my apologies and a case of Mommy's Time Out.

Thank you to the always brilliant and delightful team of Megyn Kelly and Doug Brunt. This book would not exist without them, since, I must admit, it was entirely their idea, hatched over an entertaining dinner. I look forward to executing on your next, extra idea. Wray and I will certainly pick up the bill.

A big thank you, from the bottom of my heart, to Marilou Ramirez and Rona Janowitz, who safeguard and care for my family when I'm not there. I don't know what I would do without you. Your tenderness and love is abundant and deeply appreciated. Thank you!

Of course, we could never adequately thank Briana Perez and her family for the most wonderful gift a family could ever receive. You gave us our Gem. May God bless your generous spirit.

Index

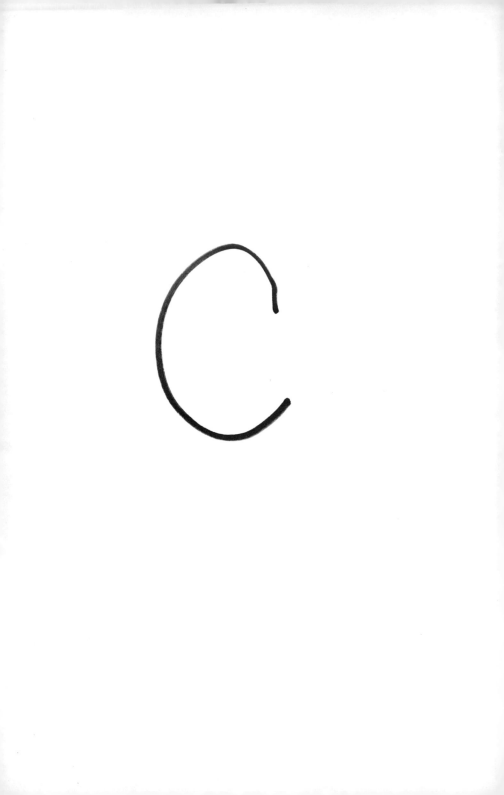